CAMBRIDGE
UNIVERSITY PRESS

Biology

for Cambridge IGCSE™

MATHS SKILLS WORKBOOK

Gemma Young

CAMBRIDGE
UNIVERSITY PRESS

University Printing House, Cambridge CB2 8BS, United Kingdom

One Liberty Plaza, 20th Floor, New York, NY 10006, USA

477 Williamstown Road, Port Melbourne, VIC 3207, Australia

314–321, 3rd Floor, Plot 3, Splendor Forum, Jasola District Centre, New Delhi – 110025, India

103 Penang Road, #05-06/07, Visioncrest Commercial, Singapore 238467

Cambridge University Press is part of the University of Cambridge.

It furthers the University's mission by disseminating knowledge in the pursuit of education, learning and research at the highest international levels of excellence.

www.cambridge.org
Information on this title: www.cambridge.org/9781108947527

First edition 2018
Second edition 2022

20 19 18 17 16 15 14 13 12 11 10 9 8 7 6 5 4 3 2 1

Printed in Italy by L.E.G.O. S.p.A.

A catalogue record for this publication is available from the British Library

ISBN 978-1-108-94752-7 Maths Skills Workbook with Digital Access (2 Years)

Additional resources for this publication at www.cambridge.org/go

DEDICATED TEACHER AWARDS

Teachers play an important part in shaping futures. Our Dedicated Teacher Awards recognise the hard work that teachers put in every day.

Thank you to everyone who nominated this year; we have been inspired and moved by all of your stories. Well done to all of our nominees for your dedication to learning and for inspiring the next generation of thinkers, leaders and innovators.

Congratulations to our incredible winners!

WINNER

Regional Winner Middle East & North Africa	Regional Winner Europe	Regional Winner North & South America	Regional Winner Central & Southern Africa	Regional Winner Australia, New Zealand & South-East Asia	Regional Winner East & South Asia
Annamma Lucy	Anna Murray	Melissa Crosby	Nonhlanhla Masina	Peggy Pesik	Raminder Kaur Mac
GEMS Our Own English High School, Sharjah - Boys' Branch, UAE	British Council, France	Frankfort High School, USA	African School for Excellence, South Africa	Sekolah Buin Batu, Indonesia	Choithram School, India

For more information about our dedicated teachers and their stories, go to
dedicatedteacher.cambridge.org

CAMBRIDGE
UNIVERSITY PRESS

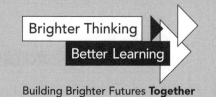

Brighter Thinking
Better Learning

Building Brighter Futures **Together**

> Contents

> How to use this series

We offer a comprehensive, flexible array of resources for the Cambridge IGCSE™ Biology syllabus. We provide targeted support and practice for the specific challenges we've heard that students face: learning science with English as a second language; learners who find the mathematical content within science difficult; and developing practical skills.

The coursebook provides coverage of the full Cambridge IGCSE Biology syllabus. Each chapter explains facts and concepts, and uses relevant real-world examples of scientific principles to bring the subject to life. Together with a focus on practical work and plenty of active learning opportunities, the coursebook prepares learners for all aspects of their scientific study. At the end of each chapter, examination-style questions offer practice opportunities for learners to apply their learning.

The digital teacher's resource contains detailed guidance for all topics of the syllabus, including common misconceptions identifying areas where learners might need extra support, as well as an engaging bank of lesson ideas for each syllabus topic. Differentiation is emphasised with advice for identification of different learner needs and suggestions of appropriate interventions to support and stretch learners. The teacher's resource also contains support for preparing and carrying out all the investigations in the practical workbook, including a set of sample results for when practicals aren't possible.

The teacher's resource also contains scaffolded worksheets and unit tests for each chapter. Answers for all components are accessible to teachers for free on the Cambridge GO platform.

The skills-focused workbook has been carefully constructed to help learners develop the skills that they need as they progress through their Cambridge IGCSE Biology course, providing further practice of all the topics in the coursebook. A three-tier, scaffolded approach to skills development enables students to gradually progress through 'focus', 'practice' and 'challenge' exercises, ensuring that every learner is supported. The workbook enables independent learning and is ideal for use in class or as homework.

The practical workbook provides learners additional opportunities for hands-on practical work, giving them full guidance and support that will help them to develop their investigative skills. These skills include planning investigations, selecting and handling apparatus, creating hypotheses, recording and displaying results, and analysing and evaluating data.

Mathematics is an integral part of scientific study, and one that learners often find a barrier to progression in science. The Maths Skills for Cambridge IGCSE Biology write-in workbook has been written in collaboration with the Association for Science Education, with each chapter focusing on several maths skills that students need to succeed in their Biology course.

Our research shows that English language skills are the single biggest barrier to students accessing international science. This write-in English language skills workbook contains exercises set within the context of Cambridge IGCSE Biology topics to consolidate understanding and embed practice in aspects of language central to the subject. Activities range from practising using 'effect' and 'affect' in the context of enzymes, to writing about expiration with a focus on common prefixes.

> How to use this book

Throughout this book, you will notice lots of different features that will help your learning.

OVERVIEW

This sets the scene for each chapter, and explains why the maths skills in that chapter are important for you to understand.

WORKED EXAMPLES

These show a maths concept in action, giving you a step-by-step guide to answering a question related to that concept.

LOOK OUT

The information in these boxes will help you complete the questions, and give you support in areas that you might find difficult.

Questions

Questions give you a chance to practise the skills in each Maths focus. You can find the answers to these questions in the Teacher's Resource.

EXAM-STYLE QUESTIONS

Questions at the end of each chapter provide more demanding exam-style questions. Answers to these questions can be found in the Teacher's Resource.

Applying more than one skill

At the end of this Workbook you will find a section of exam-style questions covering any of the topics covered in the chapters. This will give you a chance to think about how to apply your maths skills to different contexts.

Throughout the book, you will see important words in **bold** font. You can find definitions for these words in the Glossary at the back of the book. Command words that appear in the syllabus and might be used in exams are also highlighted in the exam-style questions. In the margin, you will find the Cambridge International definition.

> Supplement content

Where content is intended for students who are studying the Supplement content of the syllabus as well as the Core, this is indicated with the arrow and bar, as you can see on the left here.

⟩ Introduction

This workbook has been written to help you to improve your skills in the mathematical processes that you need in your Cambridge IGCSE™ Biology course. The exercises will guide you and give you practice in:

- representing values
- working with data
- drawing graphs and charts
- interpreting data
- doing calculations
- working with shape.

Each chapter focuses on several maths skills that you will need in your biology course. It explains why you need these skills. Then, for each skill, it presents a step-by-step worked example of a question that involves the skill. This is followed by questions for you to try. They are not like exam questions. They are designed to develop your skills and understanding; they get increasingly challenging. Tips are often given alongside to guide you. Spaces, lines or graph grids are provided for your answers. In biology, there are lots of contexts where maths is used. You will be calculating magnification and using scale when working with microscopes. Probability and ratio are used to interpret the results from genetic crosses. An important skill is analysing data in the form of tables, graphs and charts. This could be data that you, or other scientists, have collected during an investigation.

There are exam-style questions at the end of each chapter to give you more confidence in using the skills practised in the chapter. At the end of the book there are additional questions that require a range of the maths skills covered in the book.

Note for teachers:

Additional teaching ideas for this Maths Skills Workbook are available on Cambridge GO, downloadable with this workbook and the Cambridge IGCSE Biology Teacher's Resource. This includes engaging activities to use in lessons, with guidance on differentiation and assessment.

Answers to all questions in this Maths Skills Workbook are also accessible to teachers at www.cambridge.org/go

⟩ Maths skills grid

The mathematical requirements focus on skills that you will need in your Cambridge IGCSE Biology course. Each of the mathematical requirements have been broken down for you with a reference to the chapters in this book that cover it. This will enable you to identify where you have practised each skill and also allow you to revise each one before your exams.

	Chapter 1	Chapter 2	Chapter 3	Chapter 4	Chapter 5	Chapter 6
Number						
add, subtract, multiply and divide	■	■			■	■
use decimals, fractions, ratios and reciprocals	■	■			■	
calculate and use percentages and percentage change					■	
use standard form	■					
express answers to an appropriate or given number of significant figures		■				■
express answers to an appropriate or given number of decimal places		■			■	
round answers appropriately		■				
Algebra						
recognise and use direct and inverse proportion				■		
solve simple algebraic equations for any one term when the other terms are known						
substitute physical quantities into a formula					■	■

	Chapter 1	Chapter 2	Chapter 3	Chapter 4	Chapter 5	Chapter 6
Geometry and measurements						
convert between units, including cm³ and dm³, mg, g and kg, µm, mm, cm and m					■	■
understand the meaning of angle, curve, circle, radius, diameter, circumference, square, rectangle and diagonal			■	■		■
recall and use equations for the area of a rectangle, the area of a triangle and the area of a circle						■
recall and use equations for the volume of a rectangular block and the volume of a cylinder						■
use a ruler	■	■			■	
make estimates of numbers, quantities and lengths	■	■	■	■		■
understand surface area and use surface area : volume ratio						■
use scale diagrams					■	
select and use the most appropriate units for recording data and the results of calculations	■		■		■	■
Graphs, charts and statistics						
draw charts and graphs from data		■				
interpret line graphs, bar charts, pie charts and histograms with equal intervals				■		
interpolate and extrapolate from data				■		
determine the gradient and intercept of a graph, including units where appropriate				■		
select suitable scales and axes for graphs				■		
recognise direct and inverse proportionality from a graph				■		
calculate the mean and range of a set of values		■				
use simple probability					■	

› Chapter 1

Representing values

Maths focus 1: Using units

KEY WORDS

derived unit: a unit made up of other units; for example, concentration can be measured in grams per cm³ (g/cm³)

symbol: a shorter version of a unit name; for example, cm is the symbol for centimetre

unit: a standard used in measuring a variable; for example, the metre or the volt

A biologist measured the length and mass of the fish in Figure 1.1.

She wrote down the measurements as 64 cm and 10.9 kg.

Figure 1.1: A type of fish called a carp.

When taking measurements in biology, it is important to choose a suitable **unit**.

The measuring apparatus you use can help you decide what units to use. The biologist used a tape measure that measured length in centimetres and a balance that measured mass in kilograms.

It is also correct to say that the fish has a length of 0.00064 km and a mass of 10 900 g, but the biologist did not use these units because the numbers are either very small or very large. This makes the measurements harder to understand.

What maths skills do you need to be able to use units?

1	Choosing the correct unit	• Consider what measuring apparatus is being used and what the apparatus is measuring.
		• Choose the most suitable unit.
2	Using unit **symbols**	• Decide what the unit is.
		• Write the correct symbol.
3	Using **derived units**	• Identify the units being used.
		• Decide what the calculation is.
		• Work out the derived unit.

Maths skills practice

KEY WORDS

meniscus: the curved surface of a liquid in a tube or cylinder

volume: a measure of three-dimensional space; measured in cubic units, for example cm^3 or m^3

How and when do you use units in practical biology?

When doing practical work in biology, you will use apparatus to make measurements and collect data. It is important that you record this data using an appropriate unit.

For example, if you measure the length of a leaf and record it as 5, it is not clear whether you mean 5 mm or 5 cm. As the difference in length is significant, your results will not be understood correctly.

It is vital that you use the correct measuring equipment. For example, you would use a ruler marked in millimetres to measure the length of a leaf. This will allow you to give a more accurate measurement than a metre ruler marked only in centimetres.

Maths skill 1: Choosing the correct unit

Table 1.1 shows some of the common measurements used in biology, along with the apparatus that scientists use to take the measurements and the units that you use for these measurements.

Measurement	Apparatus	Unit
length/width	ruler, tape measure	millimetres, centimetres, metres
mass	balance	grams, kilograms
volume	measuring cylinder, pipette	cubic centimetres
temperature	thermometer	degrees Celsius
time	stop-clock	seconds

Table 1.1: Common measurements and apparatus used in biology.

LOOK OUT

Remember, mass is measured in kilograms (or grams). Weight is a force measured in newtons.

WORKED EXAMPLE 1.1

A student investigates transpiration using a potometer. Figure 1.2 shows the apparatus she uses.

See Experimental skills 8.2 in the Coursebook for more information on how to use a potometer.

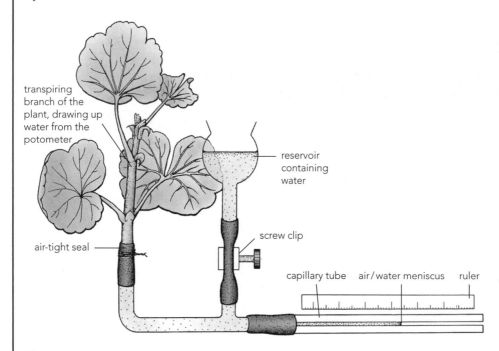

transpiring branch of the plant, drawing up water from the potometer

reservoir containing water

screw clip

air-tight seal

capillary tube   air / water meniscus   ruler

Figure 1.2: A potometer.

CONTINUED

The student uses a ruler to measure the distance that the **meniscus** moves in 5 minutes. The ruler has divisions in both centimetres and millimetres.

1 centimetre   1 millimetre

Figure 1.3: A ruler divided into millimetres and centimetres.

Which unit should the student use to measure the distance?

Key questions to ask yourself:

- What measuring apparatus is being used?
- What is the apparatus measuring?
- What are the units of the divisions on the apparatus?
- Which unit is the most appropriate to use?

It would be a mistake to use metres as the unit because the values would be too small. The student should choose a unit that will produce numbers that are not too small and not too large.

The student should use millimetres. She could also use centimetres, although this would mean her data contain a decimal point.

Questions

1 A biologist is investigating variation in physical characteristics in humans. He asks a person to step onto some scales.

   a What measurement is the biologist taking?

      ....

   b What would be the most appropriate unit to use?

      ....

2 A student investigates how the height of a seedling changes over time. She decides to measure the height of the seedling in metres.

   a Why would metres not be a good choice of unit to measure the height of the seedling?

      ....

   b Suggest a suitable unit.

      ....

Maths skill 2: Using unit symbols

Instead of writing out the unit name each time, you can use a shorter version called a symbol (see Table 1.2).

Make sure you use the correct case for the letters in the symbols. For example, cm for centimetres is written in lower-case letters, but °C for degrees Celsius is an upper-case letter. Other units, for example kJ (kilojoules), contain both lower-case and upper-case letters.

Unit	Symbol	Unit	Symbol
metre	m	gram	g
centimetre	cm	degrees Celsius	°C
millimetre	mm	cubic centimetre	cm³
kilogram	kg	second	s

Table 1.2: Some units and their symbols.

There are many more units used in biology than the ones in the table. These are formed by using derived units (see Maths skill 3) or unit prefixes.

WORKED EXAMPLE 1.2

A student did an osmosis experiment. The student cut up a potato into small cubes with sides of equal length. The student then placed the cubes into test-tubes, each containing the same volume of salt solution.

You can read more about this experiment in Chapter 3 of the Coursebook and Workbook.

What measurements did the student take when he was setting up the experiment? What units should the student use for each measurement?

Length of sides of potato cube: the student should use millimetres (mm).

Volume of salt solution: the student should use cubic centimetres (cm³).

Questions

3   Using Table 1.2, write down the unit symbol that you would use for each of the following measurements:

   a   volume of water measured using a pipette

   ....

   b   thickness of a leaf

   ....

c   temperature of the room

   ....

d   time taken for an enzyme to break down a substrate.

   ....

4   Compare your answers to question **3** with a partner.

   Do you and your partner agree with all the symbols you chose in questions **3a–d**?
   Remember, for many measurements there are different units that can be used.

   If you don't agree with your partner, discuss why you choose a different unit.

Maths skill 3: Using derived units

Some units are made up (derived) from other units.

Concentration of a solution can be measured in grams per cubic centimetre, or
g/cm^3. This unit came from a calculation. To calculate concentration you divide mass
by volume:

$$\text{concentration} = \frac{\text{mass}}{\text{volume}}$$

So, the units are g/cm^3. This is a derived unit.

LOOK OUT

Note that g/cm^3 can
also be written as
$g\,cm^{-3}$.

WORKED EXAMPLE 1.4

A scientist used a microscope to study pollen tubes growing (Figure 1.4).

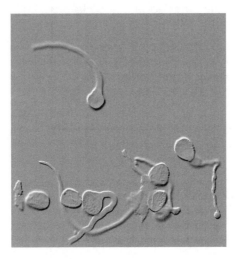

Figure 1.4: Pollen tubes.

A pollen tube grew 2.4 mm in 600 s.

What unit should the scientist use to show the rate of growth?

The scientist should use mm/s
(So, the rate of growth was $\frac{2.4}{600} = 0.004$ mm/s.)

Questions

5 Write down the derived unit for each measurement being described.

   a A quantity of sugar measured in grams was dissolved in a volume of water measured in cubic centimetres (cm^3).

   ....

   b A cat ran across a room. The time taken was measured in seconds.

   ....

6 A student investigates an enzyme-catalysed reaction.

   The student adds an enzyme to a substrate and then measures the volume of product made over a period of time.

   Identify the derived unit that the student would use to present her data.

   ....

Maths focus 2: Representing very large and very small numbers

KEY WORDS

diameter: a straight line connecting two points on the outer edge of a circle (or sphere) that passes through the centre

power of ten: a number such as 10^3 or 10^{-3}

standard form: notation in which a number is written as a number between 1 and 10 multiplied by a power of ten; for example, 4.78×10^9; also called scientific notation or standard index form

In biology you often have to use very small or large numbers.

For example:

• The **diameter** of a strand of DNA is 0.000 000 004 metres.

• There are around 37 200 000 000 000 cells in the human body.

Values written like this are hard to understand. It is easy to make a mistake and include incorrect numbers or miss some numbers out.

Also, writing them takes a long time, and a lot of space.

For these reasons biologists often use **standard form**.

Converting the values into standard form gives us:

• The diameter of a strand of DNA is 4×10^{-9} metres.

• There are around 3.72×10^{13} cells in the human body.

These numbers are shorter and clearer. It also helps you to compare the size of the numbers.

For example, 2.6×10^5 is around 100 times bigger than 2.2×10^3.

What maths skills do you need to represent very small and very large numbers?

1	Writing very large numbers in standard form	• Write the number as a number between 1 and 10, e.g. 900 is written as 9.
		• Count how many times the number has to be multiplied by 10, e.g. $900 = 9 \times 10 \times 10$ so it has to be multiplied by 10 twice.
		• Then convert the multiple of 10 into a **power of ten**, e.g. $9 \times 10 \times 10 = 9 \times 10^2$.
2	Writing very small numbers in standard form	• Write the number as a number between 1 and 9, e.g. 0.05 is written as 5.
		• Count how many times the number has to be divided by 10, e.g. $0.05 = 5 \div 10 \div 10$ so it has to be divided by 10 twice.
		• Then convert the multiple of 10 into a negative power of ten, e.g. $5 \div 10 \div 10 = 5 \times 10^{-2}$.

Maths skills practice

Maths skill 1: Writing very large numbers in standard form

WORKED EXAMPLE 1.4

Convert the number 30 000 into standard form.

Step 1: Write the number as a number between 1 and 10.

For this number it is 3.

Step 2: Count how many times the number has to be multiplied by 10 to get the original number.

To convert the number 3 into 30 000 it has to be multiplied by 10 four times.

$$\overset{\times 10}{\curvearrowright}\ \overset{\times 10}{\curvearrowright}\ \overset{\times 10}{\curvearrowright}\ \overset{\times 10}{\curvearrowright}$$
$$3 \quad 0 \quad 0 \quad 0 \quad 0$$

> CONTINUED
>
> **Step 3:** Convert the multiple of 10 into a power of ten.
>
> $$3 \times 10^4$$
>
> The 4 shows that we had to multiply 3 by 10 four times.
>
> The number is now in standard form.

Questions

7 Convert these numbers into standard form.

   a 50 000

....

   b 6700

....

   c 275 000 000

....

8 Convert these numbers from standard form:

   a 2.08×10^2

....

   b 9.25×10^5

....

   c 1.006×10^8

....

9 A colony of bacteria contains 17 000 000 bacteria.
Write this number in standard form.

....

Check your answers before you continue to the next maths skill.

Maths skill 2: Writing very small numbers in standard form

WORKED EXAMPLE 1.5

Convert the number 0.000 075 into standard form.

Step 1: Write the number as a number between 1 and 10.

For this number it is 7.5.

Step 2: Count how many times the number has to be divided by 10.

To convert the number 7.5 into 0.000075, it has to be divided by 10 five times.

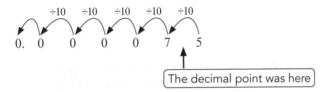

The decimal point was here

Step 3: Convert the multiple of 10 into a negative power of ten.

$$7.5 \times 10^{-5}$$

The −5 shows that we had to divide 7.5 by 10 five times

The number is now in standard form.

LOOK OUT

In standard form the decimal point is always placed after the first non-zero figure.

Questions

10 Convert these numbers into standard form.

a 0.003

....

b 0.000 060 8

....

c 0.000 000 041 08

....

11 Convert these numbers from standard form.

a 6×10^{-4}

....

b 7.22×10^{-7}

....

c 5.008×10^{-3}

....

12 The diameter of an animal cell is 0.000 105 metres.

Write this in standard form.

....

13 Which do you find easier: converting large numbers or small numbers into standard form? Why do you find this type of conversion easier?

Write some more questions for yourself and ask a partner to check your answers.

....

....

....

Maths focus 3: Using unit prefixes and converting units

KEY WORDS

unit prefix: a prefix (term added to the front of a word) added to a unit name to indicate a power of 10 of that unit (e.g. 1 *millimetre* = 10^{-3} *metre*)

When you measure mass at school you will normally use the unit grams.

However, grams are not an appropriate unit to measure the mass of much smaller or larger objects. Here are the masses of two animals, a giant tortoise (Figure 1.5) and a mosquito (Figure 1.6):

$$\text{Mass of a giant tortoise} = 200\,000\,g$$

$$\text{Mass of a mosquito} = 0.0025\,g$$

Figure 1.5: A giant tortoise.

Figure 1.6: A mosquito.

You can add a **unit prefix** to the start of a unit to change its value.

For example, the prefix kilo- makes the unit 1000 times larger. So:

$$1\,kg = 1000\,g$$

The prefix milli- makes the unit 1000 times smaller. So:

$$1\,mg = 0.001\,g$$

You can use these to convert the masses of the animals into a more appropriate unit:

$$\text{Mass of a giant tortoise} = 200\,kg$$

$$\text{Mass of a mosquito} = 2.5\,mg$$

What maths skills do you need to use unit prefixes and convert units?

1	Using powers of ten	• Write powers of tens as numbers.
		• Write numbers as powers of ten.
2	Using negative powers of ten	• Write negative powers of tens as numbers.
		• Write numbers as negative powers of ten.
3	Using unit prefixes	• Convert the number into a power of ten.
4	Converting units	• Decide if you need to multiply or divide.
		• Do the calculation. Remember to add units to your answer.
		• Check that the size of the answer looks correct.

Maths skill practice

KEY WORDS

index: a small number that indicates the power; for example, the index 4 shows that the 2 is raised to the power 4, which means four 2s multiplied together: $2^4 = 2 \times 2 \times 2 \times 2$

power: a number raised to the power 2 is squared (e.g. x^2), a number raised to the power 3 is cubed (e.g. x^3), and so on

Maths skill 1: Using powers of ten

You already know that 10^2 can be read as '10 squared' and means 10×10. Its value is 100.

It can also be read as '10 to the power of 2'.

The small number is the **power** or **index**. It shows how many times we multiply by 10; see Table 1.3.

The number of zeros in the value is the same as the power. So 10^2 is 100, which shows that 1 has been multiplied by 10 two times.

Power of ten	Multiplying tens	Value	Name
10^0	–	1	one
10^1	10	10	ten
10^2	10×10	100	one hundred
10^3	$10 \times 10 \times 10$	1000	one thousand
10^4	$10 \times 10 \times 10 \times 10$	10000	ten thousand
10^5			
10^6			

Table 1.3: Some powers of ten and their values.

LOOK OUT

Leaving a space between every three digits makes larger numbers easier to read. For example, one million written as 1 000 000 is easier to recognise than 1000000.

WORKED EXAMPLE 1.6

Explain why 1000 can also be written as 10^3.

$1000 = 10 \times 10 \times 10$

So, three 10s are being multiplied together.

This can be written as 10^3.

Questions

14 Complete the final two rows of Table 1.3.

15 Write the following as powers of ten:

a 1000

....

b 1 000 000 000

....

c 10 million

....

16 Write the values of the following powers of ten:

a 10^5

....

b 10^8

....

c 10^{10}

....

Maths skill 2: Using negative powers of ten

Powers of ten can also have negative values.

Table 1.4 shows how these are calculated.

Power of ten	Dividing tens	Value	Name
10^{-1}	$1 \div 10$	0.1	one tenth
10^{-2}	$1 \div (10 \times 10)$	0.01	one hundredth
10^{-5}	$1 \div (10 \times 10 \times 10 \times 10 \times 10)$	0.00001	one hundred thousandth
10^{-6}	$1 \div (10 \times 10 \times 10 \times 10 \times 10 \times 10)$	0.000001	one millionth

Table 1.4: Calculating negative powers of ten.

The negative index or power of ten tells you how many times to divide by 10:

$$10^{-2} \text{ is } \frac{1}{10 \times 10} = \frac{1}{100}$$

$$10^{-5} \text{ is } \frac{1}{10 \times 10 \times 10 \times 10 \times 10} = \frac{1}{100\,000}$$

WORKED EXAMPLE 1.7

Explain why 0.01 can also be written as 10^{-2}.

$0.01 = 1 \div 100$

So, $0.01 = 1 \div 10^2$.

This can be written as 10^{-2}.

Questions

17 Complete the missing two rows of Table 1.4.

18 Write the following values as powers of ten:

    a 0.01

    ....

    b 0.000 000 000 1

    ....

    c one ten millionth

    ....

19 Write the values of the following powers of ten:

a 10^{-1}

....

b 10^{-4}

....

c 10^{-8}

....

Maths skill 3: Using unit prefixes

A prefix is added to the start of a unit to change its value.

Each prefix has a power of ten associated with it.

Table 1.5 shows the most common prefixes used in biology.

Prefix	Prefix symbol	Power of ten	Example	
			Unit name	Unit symbol
kilo-	k	10^3	kilometre	km
–	–	10^0	metre	m
deci-	d	10^{-1}	decimetre	dm
centi-	c	10^{-2}	centimetre	cm
milli-	m	10^{-3}	millimetre	mm
micro-	μ	10^{-6}	micrometre	μm
nano-	n	10^{-9}	nanometre	nm

Table 1.5: Common prefixes used in biology.

> **LOOK OUT**
>
> The symbol for the prefix micro- might look like a letter 'u' in some print, but it is in fact a Greek letter (called mu), μ. Make sure you write it correctly.

A 'nanometre' is a type of unit used for measuring length. This content goes beyond the requirements of the syllabus.

> **WORKED EXAMPLE 1.8**
>
> The length of a bacterial cell is 0.000 001 m. Write the length in metres using standard form and using a different unit with a prefix.
>
> The length in standard form is 1×10^{-6}
>
> 1×10^{-6} metres $= 1\,\mu m$

Questions

20 Write the missing unit symbol.

The first one has been done as an example.

a 10^3 metres = 1 km ....

b 10^3 g = 1 ....

c 10^{-2} m^3 = 1 ....

d 10^{-3} s = 1 ....

e 10^{-9} J = 1 ....

21 A cell membrane is 0.000 000 01 metres thick.

Write this number using a more appropriate unit.

....

....

....

Maths skill 4: Converting units

When you want to compare two objects, it is helpful to convert data so that the measurements are in the same units for both objects.

For example, two objects have the masses 0.45 g and 900 mg. Converting both of the measurements into milligrams will give you the values 450 mg and 900 mg, so you can see that the second mass is double the first.

Table 1.6 shows you how to convert units.

	Prefix	Example	Power of ten	
÷ 1000	kilo-	kg	10^3	× 1000
÷ 1000	–	g	10^0	× 1000
÷ 1000	milli-	mg	10^{-3}	× 1000
÷ 1000	micro-	µg	10^{-6}	× 1000
	nano-	ng	10^{-9}	× 1000

Table 1.6: Converting units.

> WORKED EXAMPLE 1.9

Convert $10\,\mu g$ into grams.

To convert micrograms into grams, you need to divide the number by 1000 twice (1000^2).

$$\frac{10}{1000^2} = 0.00001\,g$$

> LOOK OUT

Check your answer by looking at its size. For example, you know that microgram (μg) is a smaller unit than gram (g), so it makes sense that $10\,\mu g$ would be a small number when converted into grams.

Questions

22 Convert the following numbers:

a 1 metre into millimetres

....

b 14 g into kilograms

....

c 1200 μm into millimetres

....

23 The diameter of a red blood cell is 8 μm. Convert this into millimetres.

....

> EXAM-STYLE QUESTIONS

1 a A student investigated how caffeine found in an energy drink affected her reaction time. She decided to use an energy drink that contains 80 mg of caffeine in a 250 cm³ can.

Calculate the concentration of caffeine in the drink in mg/cm³.

....

.... [1]

> COMMAND WORD

calculate: work out from given facts, figures or information

b The student measured her reaction time five times before drinking the energy drink.

To get accurate results, she used a computer program to do this.

Her results were:

0.315 s   0.423 s   0.345 s   0.478 s   0.278 s

CONTINUED

    i   Calculate her mean reaction time in seconds.

....

.... [1]

    ii   Convert this time into milliseconds.

....

.... [1]

c   The student needed to drink a cup of the energy drink.

       Suggest a suitable unit for measuring the volume of energy drink.

       Explain why you chose this unit.

....

.... [2]

d   The student waited 10 minutes and then she repeated the reaction time test.

       The student's new mean reaction time was lower than her mean reaction time before she drank the energy drink. What conclusion can the student make from this evidence?

.... [1]

       [Total: 6]

2   A scientist counted 9856 white blood cells in 1 µl of blood.

    a   Calculate an estimate for the number of white blood cells in 5 litres of blood (the average volume of blood in an adult man).

....

....

.... [3]

    b   **Give** the answer in standard form.

.... [1]

       [Total: 4]

COMMAND WORDS

suggest: apply knowledge and understanding to situations where there are a range of valid responses in order to make proposals/ put forward considerations

explain: set out purposes or reasons / make the relationships between things evident / provide why and/or how and support with relevant evidence

give: produce an answer from a given source or recall/memory

> Chapter 2

Working with data

WHY DO YOU NEED TO WORK WITH DATA IN BIOLOGY?

- In biology, you will do many investigations and gather data as evidence.

- Data must be collected accurately to reduce the number of errors.

- Data are usually recorded in a results table. This allows you to see patterns more clearly in the data so you can draw conclusions.

Maths focus 1: Naming types of data

KEY WORDS

categorical data: data that can be grouped into categories (types) but not ordered

continuous data: data that can take any numerical value within a range

control variable: a variable that is kept constant in an investigation

dependent variable: the variable that is measured or observed in an investigation, when the independent variable is changed

discrete data: data that can take only certain values

independent variable: a variable in an investigation that is changed by the experimenter

qualitative data: data that are descriptive and not numerical

quantitative data: data that are numerical

variable: a factor that is measured, changed or controlled in an experiment

Whenever an investigation is carried out in biology, **variables** (factors that can be measured, controlled or changed) are used. One variable is chosen to be changed. This is the **independent variable**.

One variable will be measured. This is the **dependent variable**. This is recorded in the results table.

All the other variables are kept the same. This ensures that the test is fair. These are **control variables**.

Data may be recorded as words, or as numbers:

- **categorical data:** where the data can be sorted into categories (groups) but the categories cannot be easily ordered; for example, the names of animals

- **continuous data:** where the data can take any value within a certain range; for example, the temperature of an object

- **discrete data:** where the data can only take certain values; for example, the number of petals on a flower can only be whole numbers.

Data can also be broadly grouped as:

- **quantitative data:** where counts or measurements are taken and recorded as values; for example, height in metres

- **qualitative data:** where descriptions are recorded; for example, names of animals or colour of eyes.

Naming the types of data will help you to decide how to arrange the data in a results table and also what type of chart or graph to use to display the data.

What maths skills do you need when naming types of data?

1	Identifying independent and dependent variables	•	Identify the variable that is changed: this is the independent variable.
		•	Identify the variable that is measured: this is the dependent variable.
2	Identifying types of data	•	Decide if the data are recorded as words or not; if the data are words, then they are categorical data.
		•	If the data are recorded as numbers, decide if the data can take any value. If they can, they are continuous data; if the data can only take certain values, they are discrete data.

Maths skills practice

How does identifying types of data relate to displaying data in biology?

Data can be displayed in a results table.

The independent variable goes in the first column and the dependent variable goes in the second column:

Name of independent variable goes here	Name of dependent variable goes here

When drawing a chart or graph, the independent variable goes on the horizontal axis (*x*-axis), and the dependent variable goes on the vertical axis (*y*-axis); see Figure 2.1.

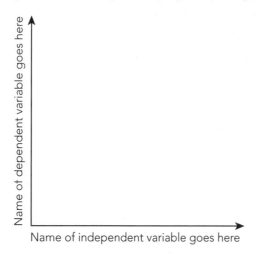

Figure 2.1: How to plot the variables on a graph.

Whether the data are categorical, discrete or continuous will help you to decide what type of chart or graph to draw.

- If the independent variable is *categorical* or *discrete* then you should use a **bar chart**.

- If the independent variable is *continuous* then you should use a **line graph**.

See Maths focus 3, Recording and processing data, to learn more about how to record data in tables.

You can find out more about drawing charts and graphs in Chapter 3, Drawing graphs and charts.

Maths skill 1: Identifying independent and dependent variables

WORKED EXAMPLE 2.1

Two students carried out an investigation to see how different types of exercise affected heart rate.

The students ran on the spot, skipped, or did star jumps for 1 minute. They measured the increase in their heart rate in beats per minute.

What variables did the students use?

Key questions to ask yourself:

- What variable did the students change? This is the *independent* variable.

- What variable did the students measure? This is the *dependent* variable.

The variable the students changed was the type of exercise they did. This is the independent variable.

The variable the students measured was the increase in their heart rate. This is the dependent variable.

Questions

1 A student investigated how pH affects amylase. The student timed how long it took the amylase to completely break down the starch.
   Draw lines to match the variable to the correct type.

Temperature of mixture   Independent variable

pH of mixture   Dependent variable

Time taken to break down the starch   Control variable (variable they kept the same)

2 State the independent and dependent variable used in each of these investigations.

    a Studying the number of measles cases in the USA every year over the last 100 years.

    ....

    b Measuring the change in mass of pieces of potato left in salt solutions with different concentrations.

    ....

    c Counting the number of dandelion plants growing in areas with different light intensities.

    ....

3 Think about how you worked out the answers to question **2**.

    a Explain to a partner how you identified the independent and dependent variables in each investigation.

    b Think of two investigations you have done. Write two more similar questions to test your partner.

    ....

    ....

Maths skill 2: Identifying types of data

WORKED EXAMPLE 2.2

Table 2.1 shows data on the mass of protein in four different grains.

Grain	Mass of protein / g per 100 g of grain
maize	10.2
rice	7.6
quinoa	16.5
wheat	14.3

Table 2.1: Mass of protein in four different grains.

What types of data are shown in Table 2.1?

CONTINUED

Key questions to ask yourself:

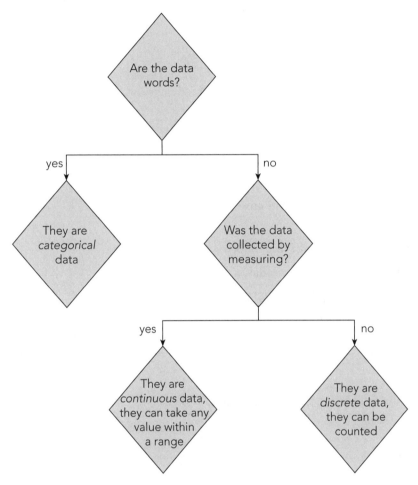

Figure 2.2: Flow chart used to work out the type of variable.

In this example the independent variable is the type of grain. The variable is provided as words, so they are categorical data.

The dependent variable is the mass of protein. The data are numbers, and they were collected by measurement, so they are continuous data.

Questions

4   A scientist collected data on trees in different forests.
     State whether each of the following are categorical, continuous or discrete data.

   a   Number of trees in the forest   ....

   b   Height of tree   ....

   c   Species of tree   ....

   d   Number of leaves on a branch   ....

   e   Width of leaf   ....

   f   Colour of flowers   ....

5   A student investigated how a variable affected the growth of cress seedlings.
     The student followed this method:

   Step 1: Place five cress seeds on cotton wool in each of four empty Petri dishes.

   Step 2: Add a different volume of water to each dish every day.

   Step 3: Measure the height of the seedlings every 2 days for 2 weeks.

   a   State the independent and dependent variables.

       Independent variable: ....

       Dependent variable: ....

   b   State if each of these variables are categorical, continuous or discrete data.
       Explain how you decided.

       ....

       ....

       ....

       ....

Maths focus 2: Collecting data

> ## KEY WORDS
>
> **accurate:** a value that is close to the true value
>
> **decimal places:** the place-value position of a number after a decimal point; the number 6.357 has three decimal places
>
> **precision:** the closeness of agreement between several measured values obtained by repeated measurements; the precision of a single value can be indicated by the number of significant figures given in the number, for example 4.027 has greater precision (is more precise) than 4.0
>
> **uncertainty:** the range of variation in experimental results because of sources of error; the true value is expected to be within this range

Data *quality* is important. If errors are made when collecting data, the results will not be **accurate**. These errors would give data that are not close to the true values. The difference between the true value and the value measured is called the **uncertainty**.

To collect accurate data make sure you:

*   use the correct measuring instrument

*   read the scale correctly.

What maths skills do you need to record and process data?

1	Choosing a suitable measuring instrument	• Work out the maximum and minimum values each instrument can measure.
		• Work out the **precision** of the instrument. This is the smallest change in a division that can be observed on it.
		• Choose the instrument that will give the most accurate measurement.
2	Reading the correct value on measuring instruments	• Work out the value of each individual mark on the instrument's scale.
		• When using a measuring cylinder, view the level of the liquid at eye level and record the volume from the bottom of the meniscus.
3	Using the correct number of significant figures	• Make sure the measurement has the same number of **decimal places** as the precision of the measuring equipment.

Maths skill practice

KEY WORDS

estimate: (find) an approximate value

mean: an average value; the sum of a set of values divided by the number of values in the set

significant figures: the number of digits in a number, not including any zeros at the beginning; for example, the number of significant figures in 0.0682 is three

How does recording and processing data help?

Figure 2.3 and Table 2.2 show some of the common measuring instruments used in biology.

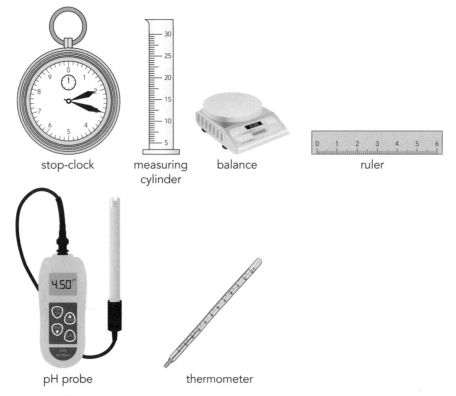

stop-clock   measuring   balance   ruler
               cylinder

pH probe   thermometer

Figure 2.3: Different types of measuring instruments used in biology.

Instrument	What it measures	Unit(s) used
stop-clock	time	seconds (s)
measuring cylinder	volume	cubic centimetres (cm³)
balance	mass	grams (g)
ruler	length	centimetres (cm), millimetres (mm)
pH probe	pH	–
thermometer	temperature	degrees Celsius (°C)

Table 2.2: What the instruments measure and the units used.

Maths skill 1: Choosing a suitable measuring instrument

When you are planning an investigation, you will decide on your dependent variable and what you will need to measure.

You will need to choose the correct measuring instrument to measure this variable. It is important to choose a measuring instrument with the correct precision. The precision is the smallest change in quantity that gives a change on the instrument. For example, most rulers are divided into millimetres so the precision of a ruler is 1 mm.

WORKED EXAMPLE 2.3

A student investigates how temperature affects the activity of the enzyme amylase.

You can read more about investigations involving enzymes in Chapter 5 of the Coursebook and Workbook.

The student is asked to measure out 5 cm³ of starch solution and 1 cm³ of amylase and place them in a test-tube. What measuring instrument should the student use?

˚CONTINUED

Figure 2.4 shows the instruments the student can choose from.

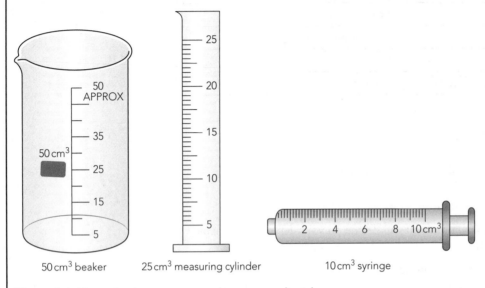

Figure 2.4: Measuring instruments used to measure liquids.

Key questions to ask yourself:

- What is the minimum volume and maximum volume each instrument can measure?

- What is the precision of each instrument?

- Which instrument will give the most accurate measurement?

The beaker would not be a good choice because measuring such small volumes in it would not be very accurate. The markings on the side go up by $5\,cm^3$ each time, so its precision is $5\,cm^3$. You could only measure a volume accurately to the nearest $5\,cm^3$.

CONTINUED

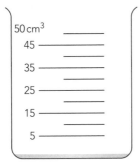

Figure 2.5: Does this beaker contain 1 cm³?

If you use the beaker to measure 1 cm³, your measurement will not be very accurate: it will have a high uncertainty. Figure 2.5 shows why.

The measuring cylinder has a higher precision (0.5 cm³) than the beaker. It will give a more accurate measurement, as long as it is used properly.

The best choice would be the syringe. This has a precision of 0.2 cm³, and so would give the most accurate measurement for small volumes.

When measuring small volumes, you should use a small measuring cylinder or a syringe. These will give you the most accurate measurements.

See Maths skill 2, Reading the correct value on measuring instruments, to learn more about how to measure accurately.

Questions

6   Which of the following instruments would be the best choice to measure 17 cm³ of water?

Give a reason for your answer.

   A   a 15 cm³ measuring cylinder

   B   a 50 cm³ beaker

   C   a 25 cm³ measuring cylinder

   D   a 50 cm³ measuring cylinder

   ....

   ....

7 Figure 2.6 shows a ruler.

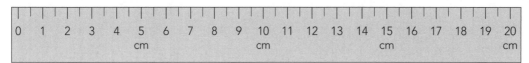

Figure 2.6: A ruler.

a What is the maximum length the ruler can measure?

....

b What is the ruler's precision?

....

c Explain why a ruler that measures in millimetres will give a more accurate measurement.

....

....

Maths skill 2: Reading the correct value on measuring instruments

Some measuring instruments are digital, for example an electronic balance or a pH probe. These instruments give you a value that you can easily read from a screen (see Figure 2.7).

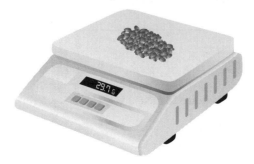

Figure 2.7: This balance has a precision of 0.1 g.

Other measuring instruments are analogue and have a scale on them that you use to read the value of the variable you are measuring. Such instruments include a thermometer and a ruler. It is easier to read digital instruments than analogue because the measurement is given to you on a screen.

WORKED EXAMPLE 2.4

Mercury thermometers are analogue measuring instruments.

They have a scale that you read to get the temperature that is being measured.

What is the temperature on the thermometer in Figure 2.8?

Figure 2.8: Reading the temperature on a thermometer.

Key questions to ask yourself:

• What is the value between each line (division) on the scale?

• What is the value of each line between the numbers on the scale?

• What is the reading?

Step 1: Work out the scale on the thermometer.

Step 2: Read the value at the top of the liquid thread.

On this thermometer, the value between each division is 10. The scale shows 0 °C, 10 °C, 20 °C and 30 °C.

There are 10 lines between each number. Therefore, the value of each line is $\frac{10}{10} = 1$ °C.

The liquid in the thermometer has reached one line above 20 °C.

The temperature must be: 20+1=21 °C.

Sometimes the level of the liquid is in between two of the lines.

What is the temperature on the thermometer in Figure 2.9?

Figure 2.9: Reading the temperature when the level of the liquid does not lie exactly on a line.

In Figure 2.9 the level is half-way between 86 °C and 87 °C.

The temperature is 86.5 °C.

CONTINUED

Because the level of the liquid is not exactly on a line the reading is an **estimate**. The actual temperature could be closer to 86.4 °C or 86.6 °C.

Care must be taken when measuring the volume of liquids. A student uses a measuring cylinder to measure out 25 cm³ of water, as shown in Figure 2.10.

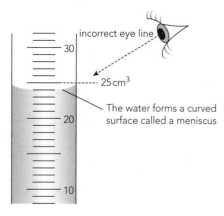

Figure 2.10: Incorrectly measuring 25 cm³ of water.

The student looks down at the level of the water and it looks like the level of the water is at 25 cm³, but it is actually 24 cm³.

When you measure the volume of liquids in a measuring cylinder you should:

- place the measuring cylinder on a flat, level surface, like a desk

- read the measurement at the bottom of the meniscus

- make sure your eye line is level with the surface of the water, as in Figure 2.11.

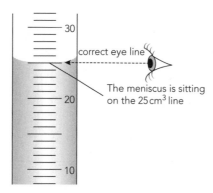

Figure 2.11: How you should measure 25 cm³ of water.

Questions

8 State the temperature reading on each thermometer.

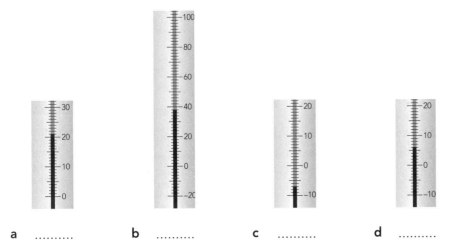

a ....   b ....   c ....   d ....

9 State the volume of the liquid in cubic centimetres (cm³) in each measuring cylinder.

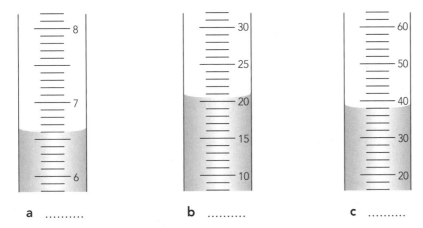

a ....   b ....   c ....

10 Figure 2.12 shows a scientist with a volume of a liquid she would like to measure.

Figure 2.12: A volume of liquid to be measured.

The scientist decides to use a measuring cylinder. Explain what the scientist should do to make sure the measurement is accurate.

....

....

....

Maths skill 3: Using the correct number of significant figures

Figure 2.13 shows how a student uses a ruler to measure the length of a leaf.

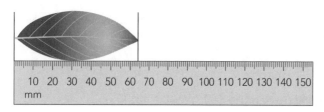

Figure 2.13: Measuring the length of a leaf.

The student writes down the length as 64 mm. The student cannot use this ruler to measure the length to a higher **precision**, for example 64.4 mm, because it is difficult to judge fractions of a millimetre on a ruler.

The value 64 mm is given to two **significant figures**. This means that the true length of the leaf is not *exactly* 64 mm but it is more likely to be closer to 64 mm than to 63 mm or 65 mm.

The student could have also written down the length as 6.4 cm or 0.064 metres. Both these answers are also to two significant figures.

The student then uses the same ruler to measure the length of another leaf. The length is 101 mm. This time the length is given to three significant figures.

When recording measurements, the number of significant figures in the data shows the *precision* of the measuring equipment.

You will find out how to use the correct number of significant figures when doing calculations in Maths focus 3, Recording and processing data.

WORKED EXAMPLE 2.5

The student then uses a digital balance to measure the mass of the leaves.

The balance measures mass to the nearest 0.01 g. Figure 2.14 shows the display on the balance.

a
$$1.22 \text{ g}$$

b
$$3.00 \text{ g}$$

Figure 2.14: The mass of each leaf is measured using a digital balance.

The student writes down the masses as 1.22 g and 3 g.

What has she done wrong?

She should have recorded the mass of the second leaf as 3.00g (so both numbers are to three significant figures). Writing 3g suggests that the scales only have a precision of 1g.

Questions

11 State the number of significant figures in each of these numbers:

 a 23 .... d 0.06 ....

 b 101 .... e 0.1005 ....

 c 4.568 .... f 1.0038 ....

12 How did you work out the answers to question 11? What rules did you follow?

....

....

....

13 A student measures his body mass.

The student uses a digital balance that measures mass to the nearest 0.1 kg.

The reading on the balance shows 82.6 kg.

 a State the number of significant figures in this number. ....

 b Explain how the student could get a more accurate measurement of his mass.

 ....

 c Describe how the number of significant figures in the measurement would change.

 ....

Maths focus 3: Recording and processing data

> ## KEY WORDS
>
> **anomalous result:** (1) one of a series of repeated experimental results that is much larger or smaller than the others (2) a point on a graph that is considered unusual compared with the trend of other values

When you do an investigation in biology you will collect data. This could be done by counting, making measurements or both.

It is important to record the data you collect in a table. This will help you to see patterns in the data so you can work out the relationship between the variables.

What maths skills do you need to record and process data?

1	Designing a suitable results table	• Write the name of the independent variable in the first column; include the units used to measure it.
		• Write the name of the dependent variable in the second column; include units.
		• If you repeated any measurements, include more than one column for the dependent variable and include a column for the **mean**.
		• Add a row for each value you used for the independent variable.
2	Calculating the mean	• Spot **anomalous results** (values that are much larger or smaller than the other values).
		• Add together the repeats (not including any anomalous results).
		• Divide the total by the number of readings.
		• Use the correct number of significant figures in the answer.

Maths skill practice

> ## KEY WORDS
>
> **range:** the interval between a lowest value and a highest value; for example, of a measured variable or on the scale of a measuring instrument
>
> **rounding:** expressing a number as an approximation, with fewer significant figures; for example, 7.436 rounded to two significant figure is 7.4, or rounded to three significant figures it is 7.44

How does recording data in a table help in an investigation of respiration rate?

The word equation for aerobic respiration is:

$$\text{glucose} + \text{oxygen} \rightarrow \text{carbon dioxide} + \text{water}$$

The rate of respiration can be measured by measuring the volume of carbon dioxide produced over a time period, such as 2 minutes. The higher the volume of carbon dioxide produced, the faster the rate of respiration.

Figure 2.15 shows the equipment that can be used to investigate how temperature affects the rate of aerobic respiration in yeast.

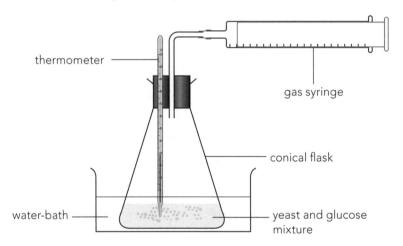

Figure 2.15: Equipment used to measure the rate of respiration in yeast. The water-bath is used to change the temperature of the yeast mixture; the volume of carbon dioxide produced in 2 minutes by the yeast is measured using the gas syringe.

The volume of carbon dioxide produced at each temperature is measured more than once, usually three times. If there are only two readings and there is a big difference between them, you would realise that one was **anomalous**, but you would not be able to tell which one it was.

Anomalous results should be omitted when calculating the mean.

Repeating measurements and calculating a mean increases the accuracy of the result because it evens out the effect of small errors or inaccuracies.

Make sure you use the term 'mean' and not 'average', because average has several different meanings.

Due to the volume of data collected, it is important to record it in a results table.

Refer to Maths skill 2, Calculating the mean, to learn more about unusual results.

Maths skill 1: Designing a suitable results table

WORKED EXAMPLE 2.6

A student investigates how temperature affected the rate of aerobic respiration in yeast using the equipment shown in Figure 2.15.

The student repeats each temperature three times and writes down the results after each measurement, as shown in Figure 2.16.

```
                    40 °C : 88, 92, 90
10 °C : 23, 21, 20
                  20 °C : 40, 43, 41
30 °C : 59, 63, 58
      50 °C : 75, 94, 77
```

Figure 2.16: A student's results.

LOOK OUT

You should always design the results table before you start collecting measurements. Use the method for the investigation to help you to identify the variables and design the table.

If someone else saw the student's results, they would find it difficult to understand what the data mean. Also, it is difficult for the student to work out any patterns in the results and draw conclusions from these data.

Therefore, the student decides to put the data into a results table. How should she do this?

Key questions to ask yourself:

- What is the independent variable? What unit is used to measure it?
- What is the dependent variable? What unit is used to measure it?
- How many different values for the independent variable did the student use? (This is the **range**.)
- How many repeats did the student make?

Table 2.3 shows how to design a results table for the data.

The name of the independent variable and the unit ↓

The name of the dependent variable with its unit ↓

Temperature / °C	Volume of carbon dioxide produced in 2 minutes / cm³			
	Reading 1	Reading 2	Reading 3	Mean
10	23	21	20	
20	40	43	41	
30	59	63	58	
40	88	92	90	
50	75	94	77	

↑ A row is added for each value used for the independent variable

↑ The measurement for each repeat is added to a different column

↑ A column is added for the mean (see Maths skill 2)

Table 2.3: How to organise the data into a results table.

Questions

14 Figure 2.17 shows the equipment some students used to investigate respiration.

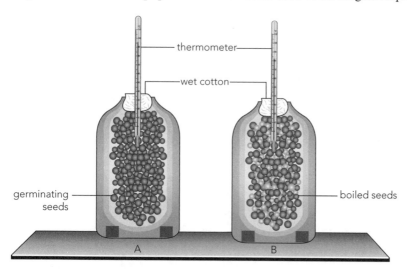

Figure 2.17: Investigating respiration of seeds.

The students displayed their results in the following table.

Type of seeds	Temperature		
	At start	At end	Rise
germinating	21	45	
boiled	22	22	0

a Identify the independent variable.

....

b Identify a mistake the students have made in designing the table.

....

c Calculate the temperature rise for the germinating seeds.

....

15 Write a checklist you can use next time you are asked to write a results table.
It should include all the things that you might forget to do, such as add units.

16 A scientist investigated how the concentration of glucose affects aerobic respiration in yeast.

The scientist measured the volume of oxygen used in cubic centimetres (cm^3) in 5 minutes.

She used glucose concentrations of $0.2\,g/cm^3$, $0.4\,g/cm^3$, $0.6\,g/cm^3$ and $0.8\,g/cm^3$.

The scientist planned to take her measurements three times.

Design a table for the scientist to record the results.

Maths skill 2: Calculating the mean

WORKED EXAMPLE 2.7

Let's return to the results table from the investigation in Worked example 2.6.

Temperature / °C	Volume of carbon dioxide produced in 2 minutes / cm³			
	Reading 1	Reading 2	Reading 3	Mean
10	23	21	20	
20	40	43	41	
30	59	63	58	
40	88	92	90	
50	75	94	77	

The next step is to calculate the mean volume of carbon dioxide produced at each temperature.

Here are the steps used to calculate the mean:

Step 1: Spot any anomalous results and exclude them from your calculation.

Anomalous results are those that are much larger or smaller than the other readings.

One of the readings for 50 °C is anomalous.

94 cm³ is much larger than both of the other readings. It is an anomalous result.

Step 2: Add together the readings.

For 10 °C the calculation would be:
23 + 21 + 20 = 64

LOOK OUT

Remember not to include any anomalous results when calculating the mean. So for 50 °C, the calculation would be:

75 + 77 = 152

152 ÷ 2 = 76

CONTINUED

Step 3: Divide the total by the number of repeats. Do this calculation on your calculator.

For 10 °C the calculation would be:

64 ÷ 3 = 21.333...

Step 4: Use the correct number of significant figures in the answer.

The mean is 21.333.... You will see that the number 3 is repeated many times. It is a recurring decimal. This is shown by the ... at the end of the number.

The value 21.333... needs to be **rounded** to the same number of significant figures as the measured result with the fewest number of significant figures. In this case all the results are given to two significant figures.

So the mean would also be rounded to two significant figures; that is, 21.

Questions

17 Complete the mean values in the table. Remember to exclude anomalous results and round to an appropriate number of significant figures.

Temperature / °C	Volume of carbon dioxide produced in 2 minutes / cm³			
	Reading 1	Reading 2	Reading 3	Mean
10	23	21	20	21
20	40	43	41	
30	59	63	58	
40	88	92	90	
50	75	94	77	

18 A student measured the mass of six grapes.

The masses were: 6.2 g, 5.4 g, 4.5 g, 4.9 g, 5.6 g, 6.3 g.

Calculate the mean.

....

EXAM-STYLE QUESTIONS

1   Some students compared the volume of vitamin C in different fruit juices.
    The students added $1\,cm^3$ of blue DCPIP solution to a test-tube.

    They counted the number of drops of juice required to turn the
    DCPIP colourless.

    a   **State** the variables the students used:

        i   independent   .... [1]

        ii dependent   .... [1]

    b   **Explain** why the students need to make sure all the drops of juice
        are the same size.

        ....

        .... [1]

        [Total: 3]

2   Hydrogen peroxide is produced by all cells. It is harmful, and must
    be removed.

    Cells produce the enzyme catalase, which catalyses the breakdown of
    hydrogen peroxide into water and oxygen.

    A class investigated how the concentration of catalase affects the rate of
    breakdown of hydrogen peroxide. They used hydrogen peroxide
    concentrations of 1 vol., 2 vol., 3 vol., 4 vol. and 5 vol. The class
    measured the volume of oxygen produced after 30 s.

    The figure shows the equipment the class used.

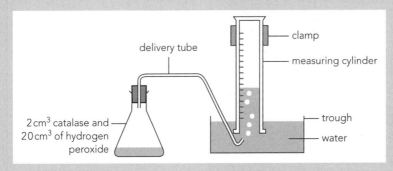

    a   The class has a variety of measuring cylinders to choose from:
        $10\,cm^3$, $25\,cm^3$, $50\,cm^3$.

        Write which measuring cylinder the class should use to measure
        the volume of:

        i   Catalase   .... [1]

        ii Hydrogen peroxide   .... [1]

        iii Oxygen produced in 30 s   .... [1]

CONTINUED

b The class is asked to take their measurements three times.

In the following space, draw a suitable table to record the results.

[4]

c The results for 2 vol. of hydrogen peroxide from one student were:

$12.6\,cm^3$, $13.2\,cm^3$, $7.2\,cm^3$

Calculate the mean.

....

.... [2]

[Total: 9]

COMMAND WORD

calculate: work out from given facts, figures or information

Chapter 3

Drawing graphs and charts

Maths focus 1: Drawing bar charts

Bar charts

Bar charts are used to show data that can be sorted into different categories. This might be categorical or discrete data.

Look at Chapter 2, Maths focus 1, Naming types of data, for more information on different types of data.

Figure 3.1 is a bar chart showing the mass of fat in different foods.

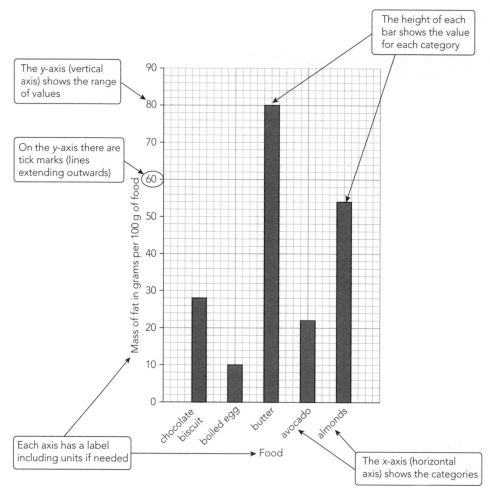

The height of each bar shows the value for each category

The y-axis (vertical axis) shows the range of values

On the y-axis there are tick marks (lines extending outwards)

Each axis has a label including units if needed

The x-axis (horizontal axis) shows the categories

Figure 3.1: A bar chart to show the mass of fat per 100 g of different foods.

What maths skills do you need to draw a bar chart?

1	Choosing a suitable scale for the y-axis	• Choose the scale so all the data can be included.
		• Aim to use as much of the graph paper as you can.
		• Avoid scales that make the values hard to read.
2	Drawing the bars	• Show each category by one bar.
		• Make all the bars the same width and separate them with a gap.
		• Draw the bars to the correct height.

Maths skill practice

KEY WORD

axis: a reference line on a graph or chart, along which a distance scale represents values of a variable

How does drawing bar charts relate to discontinuous variation?

In biology, you might collect data on variation in a group of people, animals or plants. Some of this data will be discrete. This means it can be sorted into categories. For example, a person's blood group is A, B, AB or O. This is shown in Table 3.1.

Blood group	Number of people
A	24
B	6
AB	2
O	28

Table 3.1: Number of people in a hospital ward with the different blood groups.

Drawing a chart makes it easier to compare how many people have each blood group. The data are categorical so can be displayed using a bar chart.

Maths skill 1: Choosing a suitable scale for the *y*-axis

For a bar chart showing the blood group data in Table 3.1, the *y*-**axis** is going to display the number of people.

The lowest number of people is 2 and the highest is 28.

It is always best to start the *y*-axis at 0 (unless all the numbers are very large). So, for this bar chart the *y*-axis will start at 0 and go up to at least 28.

Graph paper is normally divided up into large squares; see Figure 3.2.
Each square contains many smaller squares, normally: $10 \times 10 = 100$.

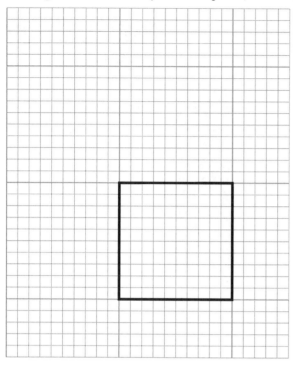

Figure 3.2: One large square on this graph paper.

The side of each large square on the graph paper should have a value. What the value is will depend on the data being presented. For example, it could have a value of 0.1 so the scale will read:

0.1   0.2   0.3   0.4, etc.

Or each large square could have a value of 1:

1   2   3   4, etc.

Or a value of 10:

10   20   30   40, etc.

The scale you choose depends on how big the numbers are that you need to show.

LOOK OUT

In some countries graph paper is also called millimetre paper, because each little square is 1 mm × 1 mm.

WORKED EXAMPLE 3.1

Look at the data on blood groups in Table 3.1. Which of the scales shown in Figure 3.3 would you choose? Explain your choice.

LOOK OUT

Make sure you leave enough space to write the title of the y-axis next to it.

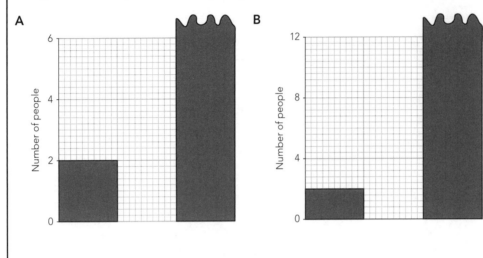

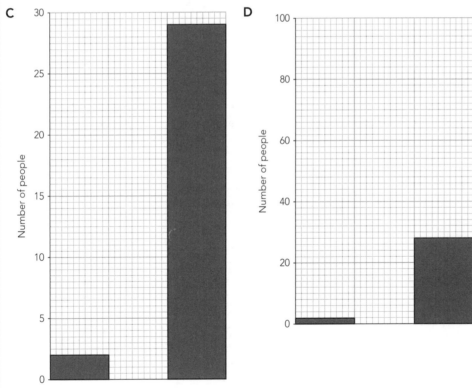

Figure 3.3: Different scales for drawing the y-axis.

CONTINUED

The scale in C would be the best choice.

This is because in A and B the bar for 28 people will not fit on the paper.

In D the bar for two people is too small to read easily. The axis with the scale you have chosen, as well as the plotted data, should take up over half of the space you have been given, whether this is a whole sheet of graph paper or the graph paper drawn on an exam paper.

Questions

1 Some people can roll their tongue and others cannot.

A teacher counted the number of students in a class who can or cannot roll their tongue.

The data are shown in Table 3.2.

Tongue roller	Number of students
yes	18
no	12

Table 3.2: Results for a survey on tongue rolling.

Which *y*-axis scale (**A–C**) is the best choice to display this data?

Draw a circle around the correct letter.

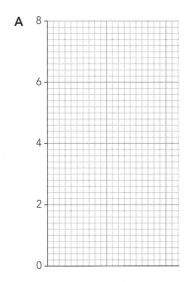
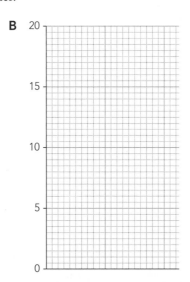
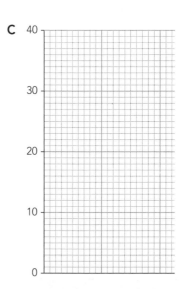

2   Arun collected data on the colour of flowers on different pea plants.

Arun's data are shown in Table 3.3.

Colour of flowers	Number of plants
white	38
yellow	20
red	14

Table 3.3: Results for a survey on the colour of flowers.

Arun writes the scale on the *y*-axis on the graph paper as shown below.

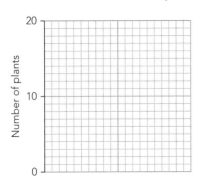

a   Explain what Arun has done wrong and why.

....

....

....

b   Suggest how Arun should draw the scale.

....

....

....

3   Shoes come in different sizes. You can only be one shoe size.

Sofia collected data on the shoe size of the girls in her class.

Table 3.4 shows the data Sofia collected.

Shoe size	Number of girls
35	0
36	3
37	8
38	6
39	6
40	4
41	1
42	0

Table 3.4: Results for a survey on shoe size.

On the following graph paper, draw a suitable *y*-axis which Sofia can use to draw a bar chart.

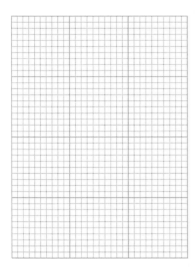

Maths skill 2: Drawing the bars

The bars on a bar chart go up from the *x*-axis.

Each bar represents one category.

The height of the bar shows the value for each category.

WORKED EXAMPLE 3.2

If we return to the blood group data from Table 3.1, we can learn the steps needed to draw the bars.

Blood group	Number of people
A	24
B	6
AB	2
O	28

LOOK OUT

The categories can also be numbers. This is called *discrete* data.

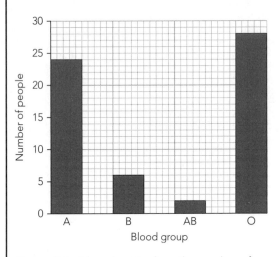

Figure 3.4: A bar chart to show the number of people with different blood groups.

Key questions to ask yourself:

- How many bars will you need to draw?

  There are four blood groups, so there will be four bars.

- How wide will each bar be? Work out how you will fit the four bars on your grid.

- How much space will you leave between each bar? Allow the same amount of space between each.

- How high do the bars need to be? Use the scale on the *y*-axis.

Step 1: Draw a line for the *x*-axis.

Step 2: Draw the bars in order of the rows in the table. For this chart, the first bar will show the number of people with blood group A. Use a ruler to draw the first bar next to the *y*-axis.

Use the scale to work out where the top of the bar should be. Using this scale, one small square represents one person. There is no need to colour in the bars.

> CONTINUED

Step 3:   Underneath the bar, write the name of the category.

Step 4:   Leave a gap and draw the next bar. The size of the gap is not important, as long as it is the same between all the bars.

Step 5:   Underneath the *x*-axis, write the label (copy this from the table). For this chart it is 'Blood group'.

Questions

4   Marcus collected data on the number of boys in each year in his school.
Marcus' data are shown in the table.

Year	Number of boys
7	120
8	89
9	101
10	117
11	95

Marcus draws a bar chart.

a   State the title of the *x*-axis. ....

b   State the name of the first bar Marcus will draw.

    ....

5   Marcus then collected data on how many boys in the school were left- or right-handed.
Marcus' data are shown in the table.

Handedness	Number of boys
right	354
left	168

Complete the bar chart to show the data.

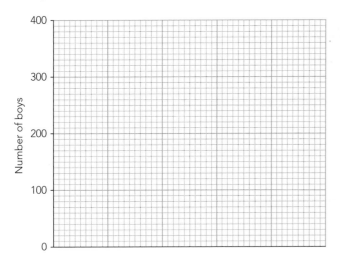

6   Marcus collected data on how many brothers or sisters (siblings) the students in his class had.

Marcus' data are shown in the table.

Number of siblings	Number of students
0	2
1	12
2	11
3	4
4+	1

Draw a bar chart to show the data.

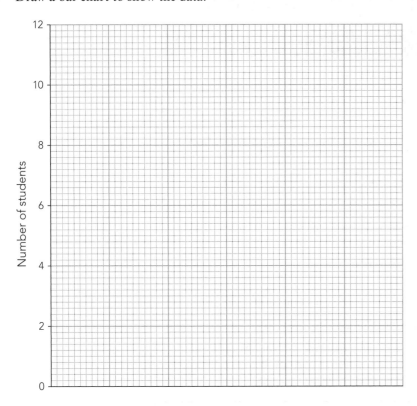

7 Here are some mistakes that people make when drawing bar charts:

A The bar chart does not fill the graph paper.

B The axes are not labelled.

C The *y*-axis does not start at 0.

D The bars are not the correct height.

Did you make any of these mistakes? Which ones? How will you make sure you don't make these mistakes again?

Maths focus 2: Drawing histograms

A **histogram** is used to display the **distribution**, or spread, of continuous data.

The data in Table 3.5 shows the masses of some bananas.

You could draw a bar chart to show the mass of each banana, but that would contain a lot of bars. Because mass is a continuous variable, you can group them together into groups called **classes**. This is displayed in a **frequency table**, as in Table 3.5.

The first column shows the classes. The size of the class is called the class interval. In this case it is 10.	The second column shows the **frequency**. This is how many bananas are in each class.

Mass / g	Frequency
110–119	3
120–129	6
130–139	5
140–149	2

Table 3.5: Frequency table of masses of bananas.

These data can be used to draw a histogram, which shows the spread of the data. Figure 3.5 shows how.

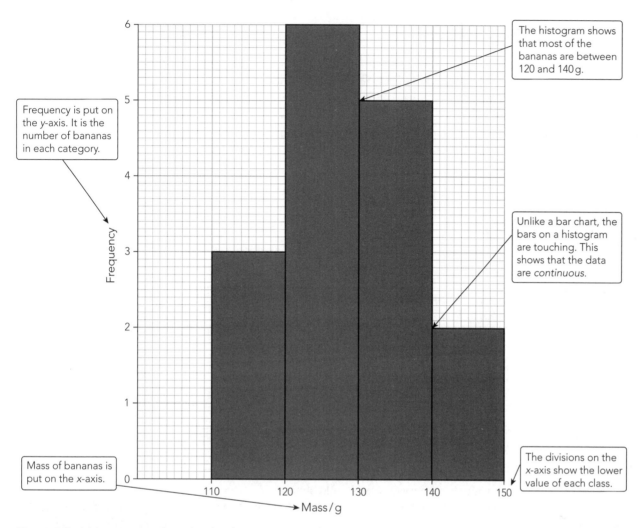

The histogram shows that most of the bananas are between 120 and 140 g.

Frequency is put on the y-axis. It is the number of bananas in each category.

Unlike a bar chart, the bars on a histogram are touching. This shows that the data are *continuous*.

Mass of bananas is put on the x-axis.

The divisions on the x-axis show the lower value of each class.

Figure 3.5: A histogram to show the distribution in mass of some bananas.

What maths skills do you need to draw a histogram?

1	Putting the data into classes	• Choose the class interval so there are neither too few nor too many classes.
		• The frequency of each class is worked out.
2	Drawing the histogram	• The classes are put on the x-axis.
		• The bars are drawn to show the frequency of each class.
		• The bars must be touching.

Maths skill practice

How does drawing histograms relate to continuous variation?

When you study variation, some of the data you collect will be continuous.
Examples include the height of plants, the hand span of people or the mass of fruit.

Maths skill 1: Putting the data into classes

WORKED EXAMPLE 3.3

The data below show the heights of a group of 15–16 year olds.

Height / cm	154, 156, 164, 151, 142, 168, 165, 170, 156, 151, 145, 142, 158, 171, 149, 165, 169, 157

Drawing a histogram will clearly show the distribution of height in the class.
This will show if more people are shorter or taller, and the most common height.
This pattern can then be compared to another class, or even the whole country.

Step 1: Write the data in ascending order.

Height / cm	142, 142, 145, 149, 151, 151, 154, 156, 156, 157, 158, 164, 165, 165, 168, 169, 170, 171

Step 2: Now you can choose your class intervals. You should choose a size that gives you neither too few nor too many classes. A total of four to six classes is a good number.

Height / cm	142, 142, 145, 149	151, 151, 154, 156, 156, 157, 158	164, 165, 165, 168, 169	170, 171
Class	140–149 cm	150–159 cm	160–169 cm	170–179 cm
Frequency	4	7	5	2

Step 3: Finally, you can work out the frequency in each class. This is how many heights fall into each class. For example, there are four students in the 140–149 cm class.

> **LOOK OUT**
>
> Your classes should not overlap. For example, you cannot choose classes of 140–150 cm and then 150–160 cm, because then it is not clear in which class a height of 150 cm would be placed.

Questions

8 The data show the length of the middle finger of a group of women.

Length of middle finger / cm	7.7	6.8	6.5	7.9	8.1	7.5	7.2	6.6	7.8	6.4	7.9	8.0	7.5	7.9	8.2

Complete this frequency table.

Length of middle finger / cm	Frequency
6.0–6.4	
6.5–6.9	
7.0–7.4	
7.5–7.9	
8.0–8.4	

9 The data show the mass of a collection of tortoises living in a zoo.
The zookeeper wants to display the data as a histogram.

Mass of tortoise / g	125	101	123	130	142	100	155	158	154	146	132	129

a The zookeeper starts to draw a frequency table.
Complete the classes in the first column.

Mass of tortoise / g	Frequency
100–114	

b Suggest why the zookeeper chose this class interval.

....

10 Zara measures the length of the leaves on a bamboo shoot.
The table shows her data, in order of length.

Length of leaf / mm	50	51	53	57	59	63	63	64	66	68	70	71	72	72	73	73

Choose suitable class intervals and draw a frequency table to display the data.

11 Here are the steps you need to follow when designing a frequency table:

Choose a suitable class size.

Write correct class intervals.

Draw the table with two columns: class and frequency.

Include units in the column headings (if needed).

Count the number of items in each class.

For each step, draw a face in the box to show how well you think you can do it:

 I can do this
really well

 I need
some help

 I can't do
this yet

Maths skill 2: Drawing the histogram

WORKED EXAMPLE 3.4

Let's return to the data we looked at in Maths skill 1, Worked example 3.3, about the heights of a group of 15–16 year olds.

Here is the frequency table for the data. We want to draw a histogram to show the data.

Height / cm	Frequency
140–149	4
150–159	7
160–169	5
170–179	2

Step 1: Draw the y-axis.

Frequency is plotted on the y-axis. Look at the highest frequency in the table.

The highest frequency is 7. Each large square has the value of 1.

Make sure you label the y-axis 'Frequency'.

Step 2: Draw the x-axis.

The divisions on the x-axis show the class intervals.

The first number will be the smallest value of your first class.

In this example it is 140 cm. You do not have to start this axis at 0.

The lowest value of the next class is 150, so this is the value you write in the next large square. Each large square in this histogram has the value of 10.

Label the *x*-axis with the variable and unit.

Step 3: Draw the bars.

The height of each bar represents the frequency of that class (see Figure 3.6).

Unlike a bar chart, the bars need to be touching. The bars don't have to be one large square wide; you can make them narrower or wider. Try to fill the graph paper you have been given.

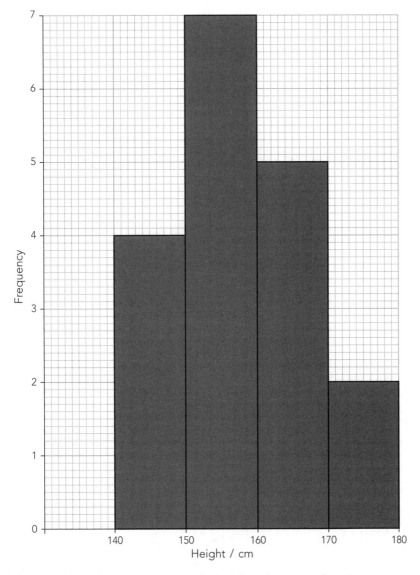

Figure 3.6: A completed histogram to show the heights of a group of students.

LOOK OUT

You should start the *y*-axis at 0.

Questions

12 Sofia collected data on the students in her class.

Sofia started with hand span. The data Sofia collected are shown in the frequency table. The data in the table use decimal numbers, but the method used is exactly the same as with whole numbers.

Hand span / cm	Frequency
15.0–16.9	2
17.0–18.9	5
19.0–20.9	8
21.0–22.9	5
23.0–24.9	3

Complete the histogram on the axes below.

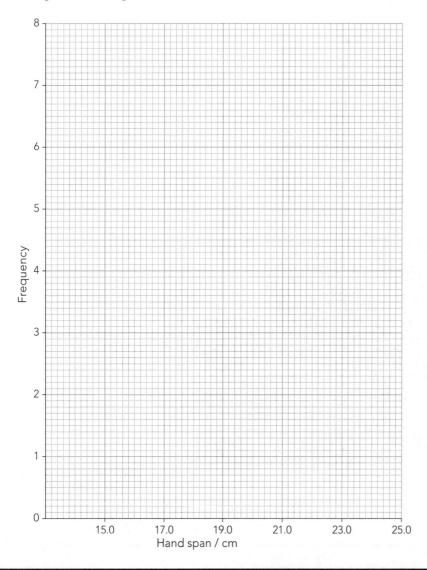

13 Sofia then measured the length of the students' right feet.

The frequency table shows the data Sofia collected.

Foot length/mm	Frequency
200–209	1
210–219	4
220–229	12
230–239	6
240–249	1

a On the graph below, draw the scale and title for the *x*-axis.

b Draw the bars to complete the histogram.

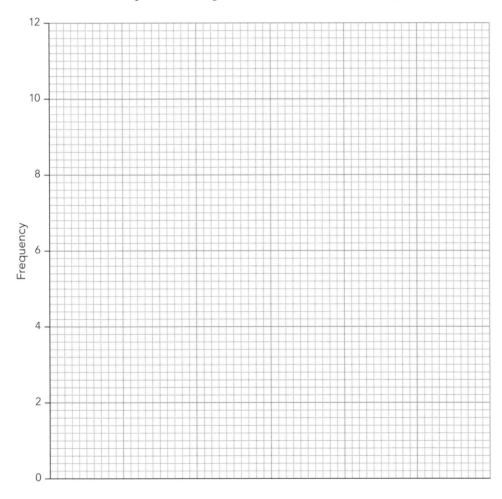

14 Finally, Sofia measured the resting heart rate of the students in her class.
The data are shown in the table.

Resting heart rate / beats per minute	Frequency
50–59	1
60–69	9
70–79	8
80–89	9
90–99	4
100–109	3

Draw a histogram to show the data on the graph paper below.

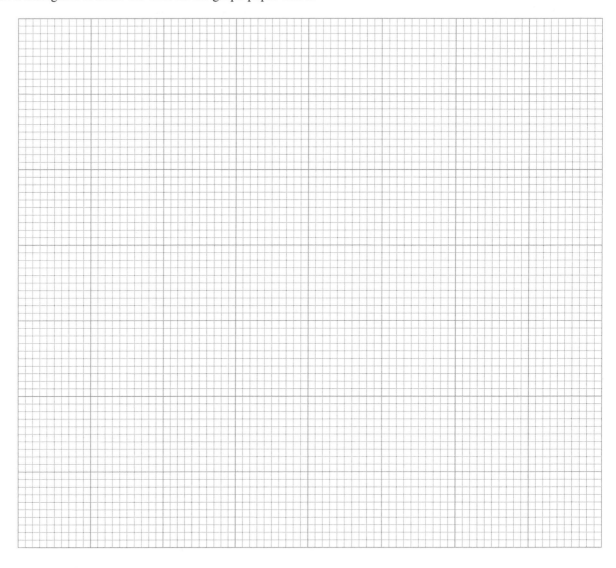

15 Swap your work with your partner.

Act as the teacher and write a comment on their answer to question 14.

Say what they have done well, and what they can improve.

16 Work in a group. Decide some continuous data that you could collect about the people in your class. Discuss:

- how you would collect the data and design the results table you could use to put the data into

- what type of chart you would use to display it, and why

- how you would draw the chart.

Maths focus 3: Drawing line graphs

Line graphs are very common in biology. They are used to show the relationship between two continuous variables: the independent and the dependent variable.

If you need reminding about the different types of variable see Chapter 2, Maths focus 1, Maths skill 1, Identifying independent and dependent variables.

For example, a line graph can be used to show how the mass of a fetus changes (see Figure 3.7).

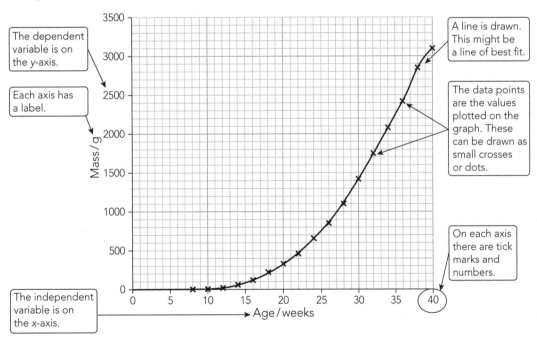

Figure 3.7: A graph to show the change in mass of a fetus.

This line graph shows how the mass (in grams) of a fetus changes with its age (in weeks).

The mass of the fetus is the dependent variable. The age of the fetus is the independent variable.

Graphs in biology can show how something varies over time. Here, time is the independent variable and so is plotted on the *x*-axis.

What maths skills do you need to draw a line graph?

1	Drawing the axes	• Decide which variable goes on which axis. • Choose the range of each axis. • Choose an appropriate scale. • Write the numbers on each axis.
2	Plotting the data points	• Accurately plot each data point.
3	Drawing the line or curve of best fit	• Know how to draw a line or curve of best fit.

Maths skill practice

KEY WORDS

best-fit line: a straight line or a smooth curve drawn on a graph that passes through or close to as many as possible of the data points; it represents the best estimate of the relationship between the variables

coordinates: values that determine the position of a data point on a graph, relative to the axes

origin: the point on a graph at which the value of both variables is zero and where the axes cross

rate: a measure of how much one variable changes relative to another variable; usually how quickly a variable changes as time progresses

trend: a pattern shown by data; on a graph this may be shown by points following a 'trend line', the best estimate of this being the best-fit line

How does drawing line graphs relate to photosynthesis?

When you study photosynthesis you will carry out many investigations and gather data.

You will investigate how different variables, such as light intensity and temperature, affect the **rate** of photosynthesis (i.e. how quickly it takes place).

Using the data to draw line graphs will help you to work out relationships between the variables. You can also calculate how they affect the rate of photosynthesis.

More about interpreting line graphs is covered in Chapter 4, Interpreting data.

Maths skill 1: Drawing the axes

WORKED EXAMPLE 3.5

Arun investigated the relationship between light intensity and volume of oxygen produced by the pondweed *Elodea* during photosynthesis.

Figure 3.8 shows the equipment Arun used.

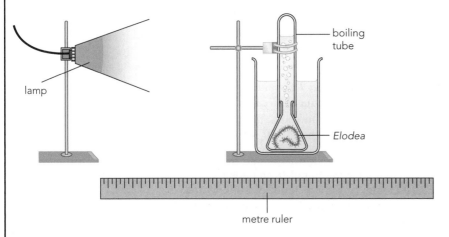

Figure 3.8: The equipment used to investigate how light intensity affects the rate of photosynthesis.

Table 3.6 shows the results.

Table 3.6: Results from an investigation into how light intensity affects the rate of photosynthesis.

Draw the axes for a graph of this data.

Step 1: First, you need to decide which is the dependent variable and which is the independent variable.

> Arun changed the distance between the lamp and the plant. This is the *independent* variable. The independent variable goes on the *x*-axis.

CONTINUED

LOOK OUT

Don't forget to label the axes, including units. You can use the headings from the table.

The number of bubbles produced in 1 minute changed as a result of moving the lamp. This was the *dependent* variable. The dependent variable goes on the *y*-axis.

Step 2: Next, you will need to work out a suitable scale for each axis. This is the same skill you learned about when drawing bar charts. See Maths focus 1, Maths skill 1, Choosing a suitable scale for the *y*-axis, to remind yourself about this. The only difference is, with a line graph, you will also need to choose a scale for the *x*-axis. You should start each axis at the **origin** (0, 0).

Step 3: Finally, you need to write the numbers on each scale. The values of the dependent variable in the table do not increase by equal amounts: 10, 20, 30, 60, 80, 100. You must not plot these values on the *x*-axis, but instead make sure each large square has the same value, such as 0, 20, 40, 60, 80, 100.

Sometimes the independent variable in a table might not be in numerical order. For example, Arun may have chosen to use a distance of 100 cm, not 10 cm, first. Even if this is the case, you must always draw the axes so they start at 0 and then increase as you go along.

Figure 3.9 shows axes suitable for plotting a line graph of this data.

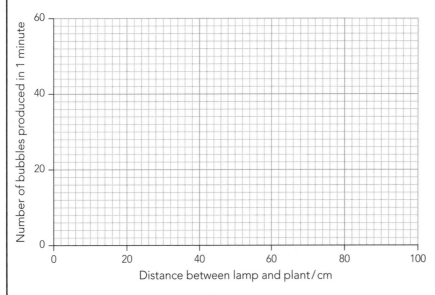

Figure 3.9: The *x*- and *y*-axes for an investigation into how light intensity affects the rate of photosynthesis.

CONTINUED

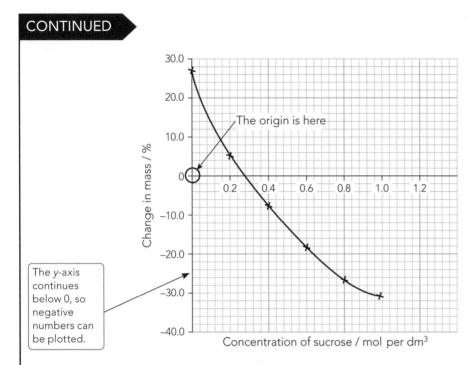

The origin is here

The y-axis continues below 0, so negative numbers can be plotted.

Figure 3.10: Change in mass of potato at different sucrose concentrations.

Questions

17 Arun investigated how the concentration of carbon dioxide affected the rate of photosynthesis.

Arun changed the concentration of carbon dioxide in the water surrounding a piece of *Elodea*. He kept the light intensity the same. Arun measured the volume of oxygen produced in 1 minute.

a What independent variable did Arun use? Circle the letter of your choice.

A Light intensity

B Length of the *Elodea*

C Number of bubbles produced in 1 minute

D Concentration of carbon dioxide

b After collecting his results, Arun decided to draw a line graph.

State what variable Arun should plot on the:

i *y*-axis: ....

ii *x*-axis: ....

18 Zara measured the light intensity (in lux) of a place in a forest. Zara took measurements every hour for a day.

The following sketch shows the axis labels for a line graph of the results.

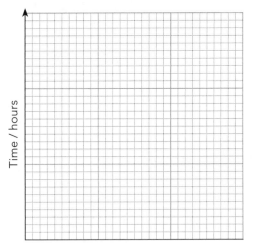

Describe the mistake Zara made in the labels.

....

....

19 Sofia investigated the effect of temperature on the rate of photosynthesis.

The table shows Sofia's results.

Temperature / °C	Number of oxygen bubbles produced in 1 minute
10	16
20	25
30	33
40	43
50	0

Complete the axes below. You should:

- decide which variable to plot on which axis

- choose a suitable scale for both axes and write numbers and tick marks on them (lines extending from the numbers to the axis)

- write labels for each axis.

Maths skill 2: Plotting the data points

WORKED EXAMPLE 3.6

Return to the data in Worked example 3.5. The first data point is in the first row of the table and is (10, 56). Each data point has an x-coordinate and a y-coordinate. The **coordinates** (x, y) show you the position of the data point on the axes. See Figure 3.11.

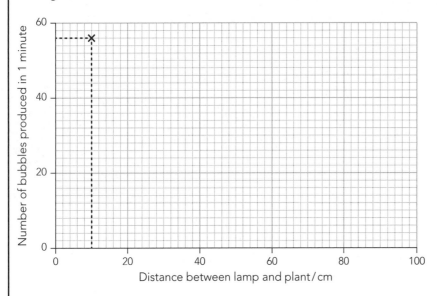

Figure 3.11: How to plot data points.

To plot this data point, find where 10 is on the x-axis and then travel up the grid line until you reach 56 on the y-axis.

On this graph paper, each large square contains 10 small ones.
To work out what each small square represents, divide the value of the large square by 10. In this example the large squares on the x-axis have a value of $20\,cm$, so the small squares each have a value of
$\frac{20}{10} = 2\,cm$.

Draw a cross or a small dot so the middle of the cross or dot is where the lines meet.

Continue until you have plotted all the data points.

Use a ruler to guide you along the lines if you find it difficult.

Questions

20 Marcus found the following results table on the internet.

Carbon dioxide concentration / %	Rate of photosynthesis / arbitrary units
0	0
0.02	20
0.04	34
0.06	40
0.08	45
0.1	48
0.12	50

Marcus plotted the data on a line graph. Circle any data points Marcus has plotted incorrectly.

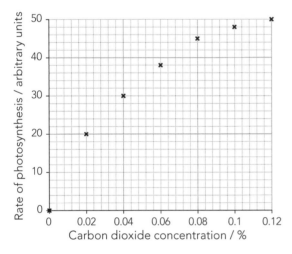

21 Arun plotted his results from an investigation on photosynthesis. Arun's graph is shown below.

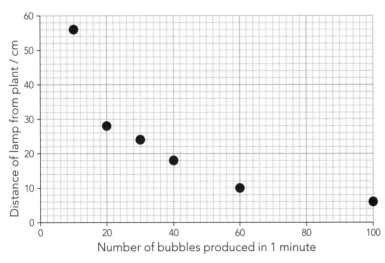

a   Describe two things that Arun has done wrong.

....

b   Explain what Arun should do to correct his mistakes and why it is important
he does.

....

....

....

....

22 The table shows some results for an investigation on photosynthesis.

Light intensity / units	Number of oxygen bubbles produced per minute
1	2
3	12
5	24
8	38
10	45
12	45

Draw the remaining data points to complete the graph. Use information from the
table above.

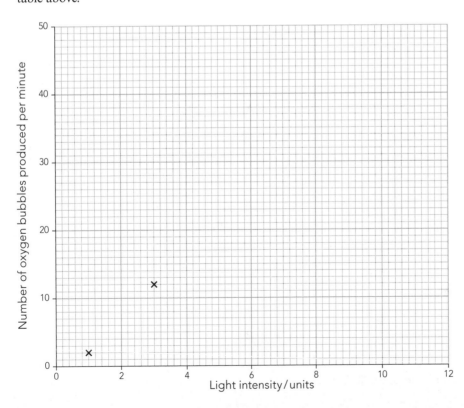

Maths skill 3: Drawing the line or curve of best fit

1   Joining the points

In biology the data you collect might be taken at intervals over time. For example, pollution levels measured once a month, or population size taken once every 5 years.

The data points should be joined. The line could be straight (see Figure 3.12a), curved (see Figure 3.12b) or go up and down in a zig-zag (see Figure 3.12c).

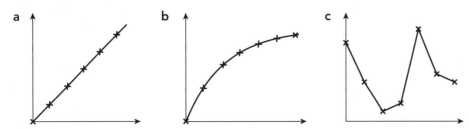

Figure 3.12: Graph **a** is a straight-line graph, graph **b** is curved and graph **c** goes up and down.

2   Drawing a best-fit line

Most of the line graphs you draw in biology are using results from an investigation where one variable affects another. The data points will not be accurate because of errors. You will need to draw a **best-fit line** to show the **trend** of the data.

Follow these steps:

Step 1:   Place a transparent ruler along the data points. This allows you to see all the points so you can judge where to draw the line.

Step 2:   Decide if the line should go through the origin (0, 0).

Step 3:   Move the ruler so there are roughly the same number of points, evenly spread, above and below the line.

> **LOOK OUT**
>
> Draw the line going through (0, 0) only if there is a data point plotted there. Otherwise, start the line at the first data point and finish at the final one.

Step 4: Use a sharp pencil to draw the line (see Figure 3.13).

The best-fit line could be a curve. The same rules apply. Try to draw a line that passes through most of the points.

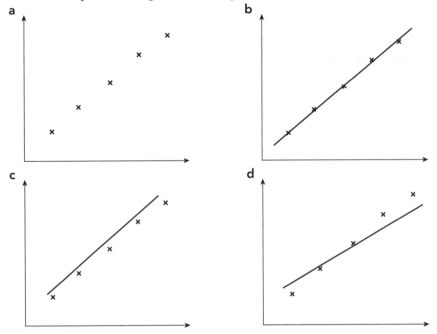

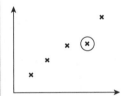

LOOK OUT

There may be one or more anomalous data points in the results. Draw a circle around them. They should be ignored when drawing the best-fit line.

Figure 3.13: The line drawn in b is an example of a good best-fit line. c and d are not good best-fit lines; in c the line is too high and in d the line has the wrong gradient (steepness).

Figure 3.14: An anomalous result.

Questions

23 Zara plotted the results from a photosynthesis investigation. Draw a best-fit line on the graph.

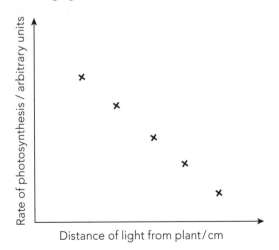

24 The graph shows the results from an investigation into how temperature affects the rate of photosynthesis.

Draw a curve of best fit on the graph.

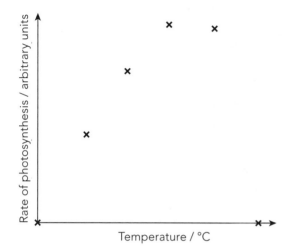

25 Draw a curve of best fit on the graph.

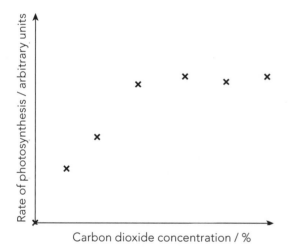

26 Write down your top tips for drawing a line graph with a best-fit line. Remember to use these tips when you need to draw a graph in a science lesson.

....

....

....

....

....

....

....

EXAM-STYLE QUESTIONS

1   A student did four different activities. His pulse was measured during each one.
     The table shows the results.

Activity	Highest pulse rate / beats per minute
sitting	67
walking slowly	75
running	98
climbing stairs	89

a   Draw a bar chart of the results on the graph paper below.   [3]

b   Estimate the highest pulse rate the student will have when
     walking quickly.

     .... [1]

[Total: 4]

CONTINUED

2   The table shows how the mass of wheat grown in a field is affected by adding fertiliser.

Fertiliser added / kg per hectare	Mass of wheat / tonnes per hectare
0	22
25	28
50	31
75	35
100	42
125	45
150	52

Draw a graph to show these data.   [4]

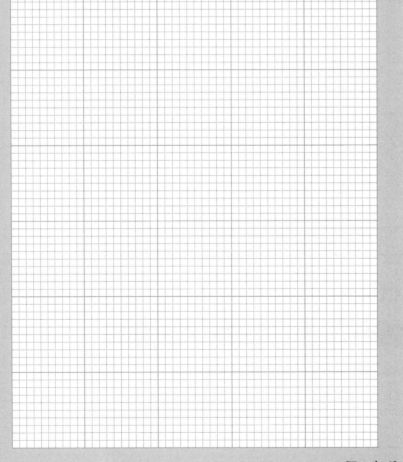

[Total: 4]

Interpreting data

Maths focus 1: Interpreting bar charts, histograms and pie charts

Bar charts and pie charts are used to display categorical data.

Histograms look like bar charts, but they show the distribution of continuous data.

The types of data are covered in detail in Chapter 2, Maths focus 1, Naming types of data.

What maths skills do you need to interpret bar charts, histograms and pie charts?

1	Identify the categories	•	Read the title of the x-axis (for bar charts and histograms).
		•	Read the key, if there is one.
2	Describe what the data shows	•	Compare the height of the bars or sizes of the segments.
		•	Use the y-axis on bar charts and histograms to read values.

Maths skill practice

KEY WORDS

percentage: a fraction expressed out of 100 (e.g. $\frac{1}{2} = \frac{50}{100} = 50\%$)

pie chart: a circular chart that is divided into sectors which represent the relative values of components; the angle of the sector is proportional to the value of the component

How does looking for patterns in bar charts, histograms and pie charts relate to human health?

Scientists collect data on large numbers of people to show patterns in health between different groups, for example, those with different ages. They represent these data in the forms of charts and graphs.

Maths skills 1 and 2: Identify the categories and describe what the data show

WORKED EXAMPLE 4.1

Figure 4.1 shows a bar chart. How do you interpret the data?

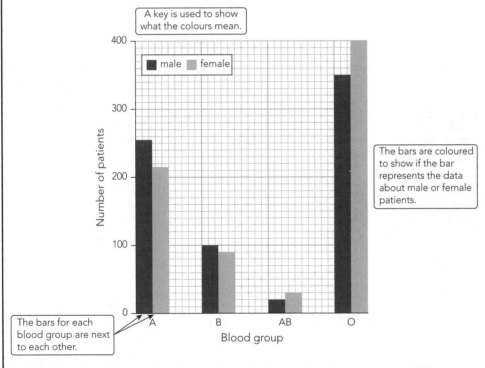

A key is used to show what the colours mean.

The bars are coloured to show if the bar represents the data about male or female patients.

The bars for each blood group are next to each other.

Figure 4.1: A bar chart to show the number of male and female patients with different blood groups.

Here are the steps you should take to interpret the data.

Step 1: Identify the categories.
Look at the title of the *x*-axis and the key (if there is one).

This bar chart has two categories.

The x-axis shows one: Blood group.

The key shows the other: whether the patient is male or female.

> CONTINUED

Step 2: Describe what the data show.

Comparing the heights of the bars tells you some information.

For example, blood group O is the most common and group AB is the least common.

Using the *y*-axis to read values allows you to discuss the data quantitatively (with numbers).

For example, for blood group A: 255 patients are male and 215 are female.

How to draw bar charts and histograms is covered in Chapter 3, Drawing graphs and charts.

> WORKED EXAMPLE 4.2

Figure 4.2 is a **pie chart** that shows the causes of premature death by illness in the UK.

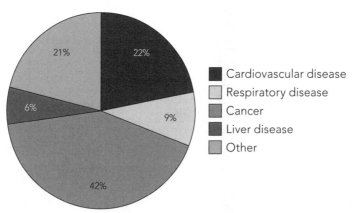

Figure 4.2: Causes of premature deaths by illness in the UK.

How do you interpret the data?

These are the steps you should take:

Step 1: Identify the categories.

Each segment in the pie chart represents one illness that causes premature death.

Step 2: Describe what the data show.

Comparing the size of the segments gives you some information.

Cancer causes the most deaths. Liver disease causes the fewest.

> LOOK OUT

If the sections in a pie chart represent percentages, then they must add up to 100%. You can use this information to calculate any missing percentages.

> LOOK OUT

Be careful when describing what pie charts show. For example, you cannot say that most people die prematurely from cancer.
It causes 42%, but the other causes add up to 58%.

CONTINUED

Using the **percentages** allows you to discuss the data quantitatively (with numbers).

Cancer (42%) causes seven times as many deaths as liver disease (6%).

Questions

1   A website has the following pie chart, which shows the proportions of foods needed for a healthy diet.

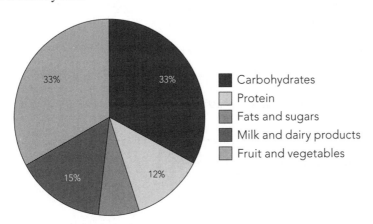

Calculate the missing percentage of fats and sugars.

....

2   A group of 100 adult men from the USA had their body mass index (BMI) measured. The histogram shows the results.

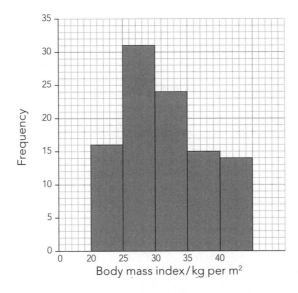

How many men had a body mass index of:

a   more than $40\,kg/m^2$? ....

b   between 20 and $30\,kg/m^2$? ....

Maths focus 2: Interpreting relationships in graphs

Line graphs are used to show how variables are related.

The shape of the graph shows the relationship, also called **correlation**.

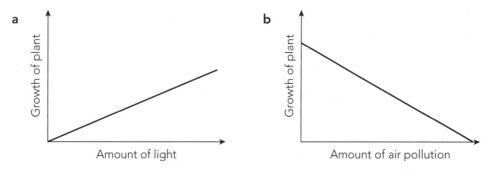

Figure 4.3: Line graphs show the relationships between variables.

In biology, line graphs often have best-fit lines. You can use the best-fit line to identify the correlation.

The graph in Figure 4.3a shows that as the amount of light increases, the growth of the plant increases. This is a **positive correlation**.

The graph in Figure 4.3b shows that as the amount of pollution increases, the growth of the plant decreases. This is a **negative correlation**.

What maths skills do you need to interpret relationships in graphs?

1	Interpreting straight-line graphs	•	Name the variables.
		•	Identify the correlation shown in the graph.
		•	Describe what the correlation shows you about how the variables are related.
2	Interpreting more complex line graphs	•	Split the line into sections, so each section has a different trend.
		•	Consider gradients and rates of change.
		•	Tell the 'story' of the graph.
3	Interpreting **scatter graphs**	•	Is there a correlation between the data points?
		•	How strong is it?
		•	What does the correlation show?

Maths skill practice

KEY WORDS

directly proportional: the relationship between two variables such that when one doubles (or multiplied by *n*), the other variable doubles (or is multiplied by *n*); the graph of the two variables is a straight line through the origin

extrapolation: extending the best-fit line on a graph beyond the range of the data, in order to estimate values not within the data set

gradient: the slope (steepness) of a line on a graph; it is calculated by dividing the vertical change by the horizontal change

interpolation: on a graph, to estimate the value of a variable from the value of the other variable, using a best-fit line; on a scale, to estimate a measurement that falls between two scale marks

ratio: a comparison of two numbers or of two measurements with the same unit; the ratio of A to B can be written A:B or expressed as a fraction $\frac{A}{B}$

Line and scatter graphs show the relationship between two variables. You can use the line to work out values not represented in the original data. This is called **interpolation** and **extrapolation**. The shape of the line shows how the variables are related.

How does looking for relationships in data relate to transport in animals?

Heart rate can be affected by many different variables, including exercise. These relationships can be identified by studying line graphs.

Coronary heart disease is a very common illness. Biologists study different variables to see if there is a link between variables and an increased risk of a person developing the illness.

Maths skill 1: Interpreting straight-line graphs

WORKED EXAMPLE 4.3

Zara carried out an investigation using water fleas.

Zara changed the temperature of the water around a flea. She used a microscope to view the heart and count the number of beats per minute.

Figure 4.4 shows Zara's results.

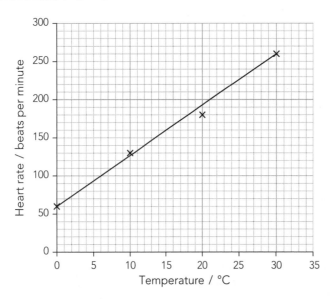

Figure 4.4: A line graph to show how temperature affects the heart rate of a water flea.

Key questions to ask yourself:

- What are the independent and dependent variables?
- Is the correlation negative or positive?
- What does this correlation show you about how the variables are related?

The independent variable is temperature; this is what was changed.

The dependent variable is heart rate (in beats per minute); this is what was measured.

The line shows a positive correlation.

So, as the temperature increased, the heart rate increased.

Figure 4.5 shows a straight line going through the origin (0, 0). The relationship is **directly proportional**. This means that as one variable is doubled (or multiplied by *n*), the other variable doubles (or is multiplied by *n*).

The **ratio** $\frac{\text{change in } y}{\text{change in } x}$ is always the same: here is it $\frac{2}{10} = 0.2$. This is the value of the **gradient**.

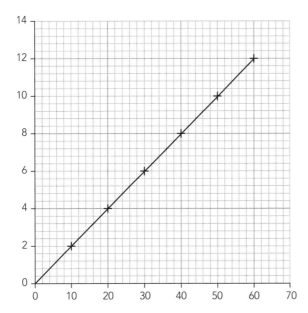

Figure 4.5: A line graph showing a directly proportional relationship. As the value on the x-axis increases by a value of 10, the value on the y-axis increases by a value of 2.

Questions

3   Marcus investigated how the concentration of ethanol affected the heart rate of a flea.

What row in the table correctly identifies the variables Marcus used?
Circle the correct letter.

	Independent variable	Dependent variable
A	Temperature of ethanol	Heart rate
B	Heart rate	Concentration of ethanol
C	Heart rate	Temperature of ethanol
D	Concentration of ethanol	Heart rate

4 The graph shows Marcus' results from the investigation in the previous question.

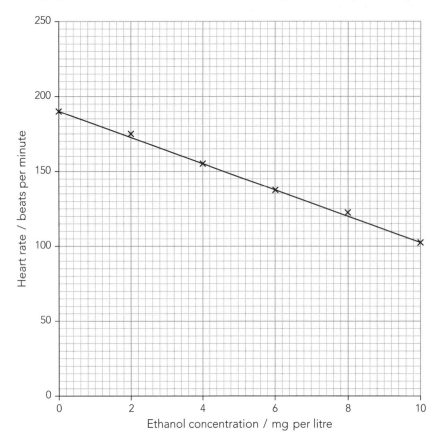

What type of correlation is shown by the graph?

....

5 Use the graph to describe the relationship between the variables.

....

6 Work with a partner. Draw a line graph that shows a positive correlation (see Figure 4.3a) and one that shows a negative correlation (see Figure 4.3b).

Think up a relationship for each type of correlation and write the variables on the axis. It doesn't have to be a biology example; a positive correlation could have the temperature of the sea on the x-axis and number of people swimming in the sea on the y-axis.

Make as many graphs as you can.

Share your graphs with another group: do you all agree on the relationships chosen?

Maths skill 2: Interpreting more complex line graphs

Many of the line graphs you use in biology are not straight lines showing a simple correlation: they can be more complex.

WORKED EXAMPLE 4.4

A man ran on an exercise machine.

Figure 4.6: A man running on a treadmill.

The graph in Figure 4.7 shows how the man's heart rate changed.

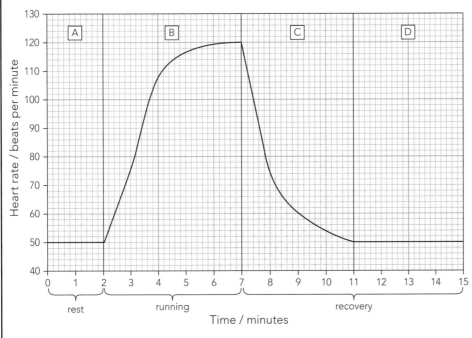

Figure 4.7: A line graph to show how the heart rate of a man changes.

LOOK OUT

You only need to consider gradient if the unit on the x-axis is a unit of time. This is because the gradient shows how the rate changes.

CONTINUED

Key questions to ask yourself:

- Can the line be split up into sections?

- Is the unit on the *x*-axis a unit of time? If so, does the steepness (gradient) of the line change?

- What is the 'story' of the graph? What is happening at each point?

This graph has four different sections. The line in each section shows a different trend. By describing the trend in each section, you can tell the 'story' of the graph.

Section A Between 0 and 2 minutes the heart rate stays at 50 beats per minute.

Section B Between 2 and 7 minutes the heart rate increases to 120 beats per minute.

Between 2 and 4 minutes the line has a steep gradient. This shows that the heart rate is increasing at a fast rate.

Between 4 and 7 minutes the gradient is less steep. This shows that the heart rate is increasing at a slower rate.

Section C Between 7 and 11 minutes the heart rate decreases back to 50 beats per minute.

Section D Between 11 and 15 minutes the heart rate stays at 50 beats per minute.

Questions

7   Caffeine is a drug found in cola. It is a drug because it stimulates the nervous system.

Arun measured his heart rate at rest for 5 minutes and then drank some cola. Arun continued to measure his heart rate at regular intervals.

Arun's results are shown below.

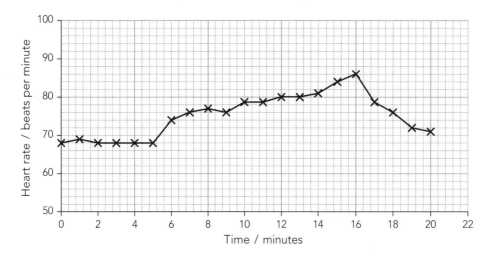

What happened to Arun's heart rate between 0 and 5 minutes? Circle the correct letter.

A It increased.

B It decreased.

C It stayed relatively constant.

D It decreased then increased.

8 Explain how the graph shows that caffeine increases heart rate.

....

....

Maths skill 3: Interpreting scatter graphs

Scatter graphs are useful for looking at the relationship between two variables from the same sample of individuals.

WORKED EXAMPLE 4.5

A scientist collected information from a sample of mammals: lifespan, heart rate and time between heart beats.

The scientist plotted the data as shown in the scatter graphs in Figure 4.8.
Each cross shows the data for a different mammal.

a

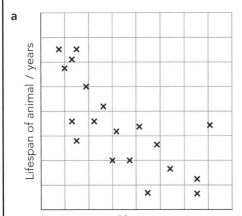

b

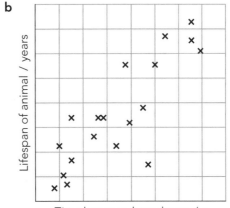

Figure 4.8: Examples of scatter graphs.

Key questions to ask yourself:

- Is there a strong correlation between the data points?

- How strong is the correlation?

- What does the correlation show?

CONTINUED ▶

The graph in Figure 4.8a suggests that there is a relationship between the lifespan and heart rate. It suggests that as the heart rate of the animal increases, its lifespan decreases. This is a negative correlation.

The graph in Figure 4.8b suggests that as the time between heart beats increases, the lifespan of the animal also increases. This is a positive correlation.

Scatter graphs do not show an exact relationship. This is why the data points are scattered: they do not all fall onto a line. The less scattered they are, the stronger the correlation.

You can draw a best-fit line on a scatter graph to show the general trend in the relationship. This could be a straight line or a curve; see Figure 4.9. See Chapter 3, Maths focus 3, Maths skill 3, Drawing the line or curve of best fit.

The best-fit line on a scatter graph has a different meaning from the best-fit line on a line graph. With a line of best fit on a line graph, the points may not all fit onto the best-fit line because of errors in measurement. With a scatter graph, it is because of differences between the individuals in the sample.

For example, in Figure 4.9 an anomalous result has been circled. This is away from the best-fit line because this individual mammal has an unusually short lifespan for the time between heart beats. You would expect it to have a longer lifespan to fit the pattern shown by the other mammals. The anomalous result is not because of an error in measurement.

If the data points are scattered with no clear correlation, it shows that the two variables are not related, as in Figure 4.10.

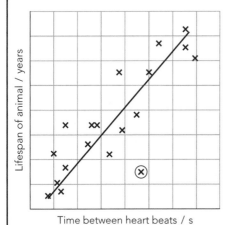

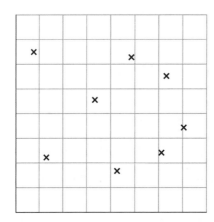

Figure 4.9: A scatter graph with a best-fit line.

Figure 4.10: A scatter graph showing no correlation between the variables.

Questions

9   Data were collected from a sample of people.

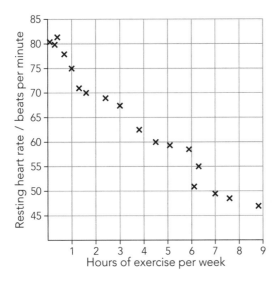

a   Draw a best-fit line.

b   Describe how strong the correlation is. Give a reason for your answer.

....

....

c   Describe what the graph shows.

....

....

d   You learned how to draw best-fit lines in Chapter 3, Drawing graphs and charts. Compare your best-fit line in part **a** with the ones you drew before.

Check:

•   you have the same number of points, evenly spread, above and below the line

•   you used a sharp pencil so there is one clear line

•   you used a ruler so the line is straight.

Have you improved?

10 Scientists collected data on how much saturated fat men ate and the death rate from coronary heart disease (CHD) in different European countries.

The graph shows the data.

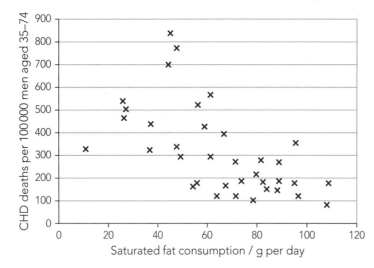

a One hypothesis is 'a diet high in saturated fat *does not* increase the risk of developing CHD'. Discuss how well the graph supports the hypothesis.

....

....

....

....

....

....

....

....

....

b Write down the steps you took when answering this question. You can use the same steps when you answer similar questions in the future.

....

....

....

....

....

Maths focus 3: Reading values from a line graph

Plotting data as a line graph allows you to estimate values between data points. This is called interpolation. It is also possible to extend the line and estimate values for higher values. This is called extrapolation.

Nitrate solution can be used as a fertiliser. Fertilisers are used to increase plant growth. Sofia carried out an investigation to see how increasing the concentration of nitrate solution affected plant growth.

Figure 4.11a shows the graph Sofia plotted from her results and interpolation; Figure 4.11b shows how Sofia could use extrapolation.

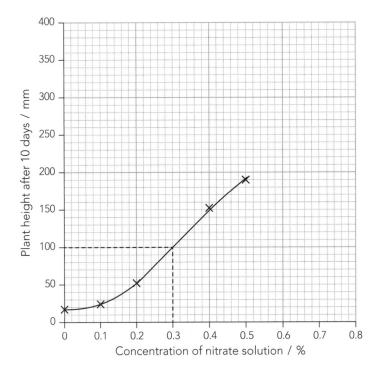

Figure 4.11a: Using interpolation.

Sofia did not use a concentration of 0.3%, but she worked out that the probable plant height was 100 mm using interpolation.

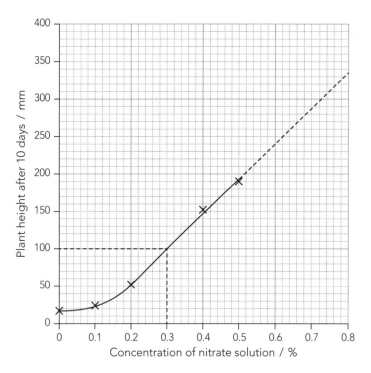

Figure 4.11b: Using extrapolation.

The highest concentration she used was 0.5%, but Sofia worked out the probable plant heights at higher concentrations by extending the line. This is extrapolation.

What maths skills do you need to read values from a line graph?

1	Interpolation	• Find the value on one axis.
		• Draw a line to the plotted line and then to the other axis.
		• Read the value from the other axis.
2	Extrapolation	• Extend the existing line.
		• Use the new line to read values.

Maths skill practice

KEY WORD

intercept: the point at which a line on a graph crosses one of the axes; it usually refers to the intercept with the vertical (*y*-) axis

How does reading values from a line graph relate to population size?

Populations of organisms can change over time. You can estimate what the population was at different times by reading values from line graphs. You can also predict what it might be like in the future.

You can find out more about population growth in Chapter 18 of the Coursebook.

Maths skill 1: Interpolation

WORKED EXAMPLE 4.6

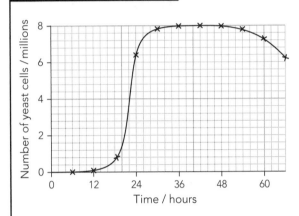

Figure 4.12: The growth of a population of yeast.

Figure 4.12 shows the results of an experiment in which yeast cells are added to a container of nutrient broth. The number of yeast cells was measured every 6 hours and a data point plotted. You estimate out how many yeast cells there were at any time between 0 and 66 hours by using interpolation.

Work out how many yeast cells there were after 22 hours.

Step 1: Work out where 22 hours is on the *x*-axis.

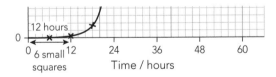

Figure 4.13: How to work out values on an axis.

The main division on the *x*-axis is 12 hours. Each main division contains six small squares; see Figure 4.13.

$$12 \div 6 = 2$$

So each small square has a value of 2 hours.

> CONTINUED

Step 2: Draw a line up from 22 hours until it meets the plotted line. Use a sharp pencil and ruler.

Step 3: Draw a line to the *y*-axis.

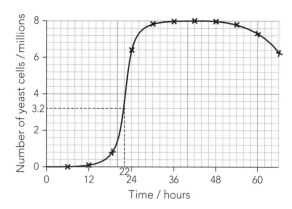

Figure 4.14: How to use interpolation.

Step 4: Work out the value on the *y*-axis (see Figure 4.13).

Each main division has a value of 2 and contains five small squares.

$$2 \div 5 = 0.4$$

So, each small square has a value of 0.4 million yeast cells.

The value on the graph is 3.2 million yeast cells.

LOOK OUT

The value worked out by interpolation is an estimate. The more measurements that are made, the more accurate the estimate will be.

Questions

11 State the value, X, on the graph.

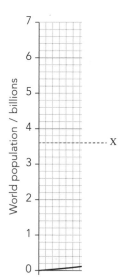

12 The graph shows the population growth of a species of bacteria.

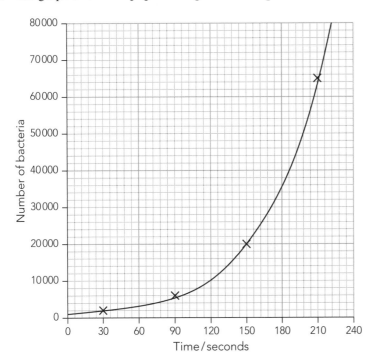

Estimate the number of bacteria after 2 minutes. ....

13 The graph shows the growth in numbers of aphids on soya bean plants in a field in North America.

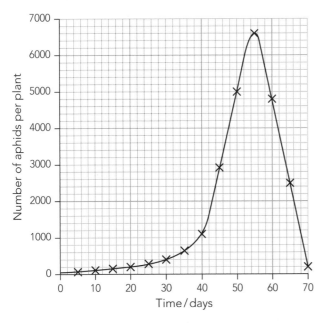

a After how many days did the population first reach 6000 aphids per plant?

....

b Explain to a partner how you worked out the answer to the question.

Maths skill 2: Extrapolation

WORKED EXAMPLE 4.7

The human population has changed over time. Figure 4.15 shows this.

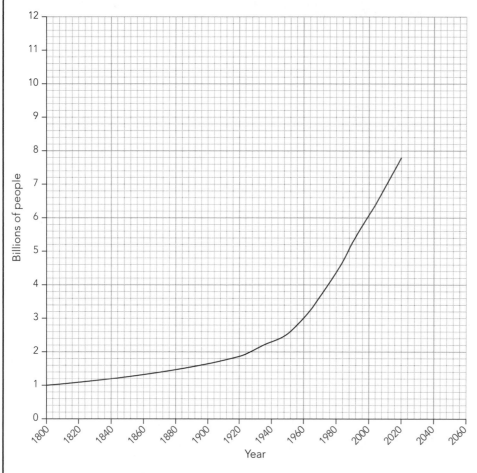

Figure 4.15: The growth of human population on Earth.

You can estimate what the population will be in the future by extending the line. This is called extrapolation. Estimate the population by the year 2060.

CONTINUED

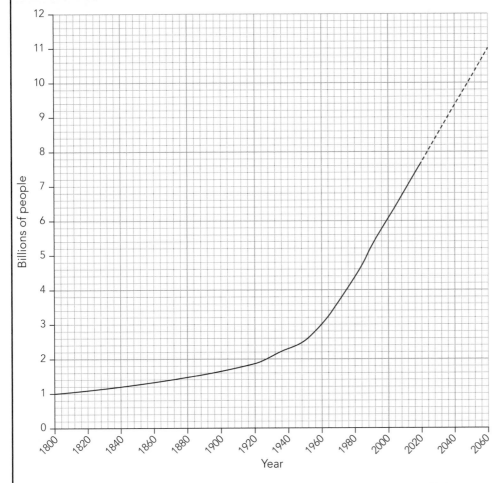

Figure 4.16: Extending the line shows an estimate of how human population will change in the future.

LOOK OUT

Take care when using extrapolation. You are assuming that the correlation stays the same outside the data range. This might not always be the case. Changes may happen in the future which result in a slower or faster population growth. The estimate is based on assuming that the rate of population change stays the same.

Step 1: Use a ruler and place it along the existing line.

Step 2: Draw a new line up, extending the line (see Figure 4.16).

This extrapolation shows that human population could reach 11 billion by 2060.

Extrapolation can also be used to extend the line towards lower values. You can use this to find out where the line crosses the *x*- or *y*-axis. This is called the **intercept**.

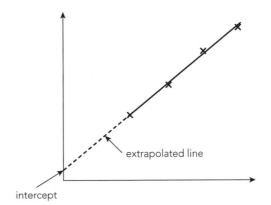

Figure 4.17: Extrapolation by extending the line towards lower values.

Questions

14 Use a ruler to extrapolate these lines:

a to higher values   **b** to higher values   **c** to lower values

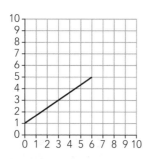 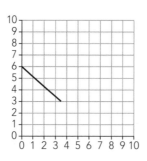 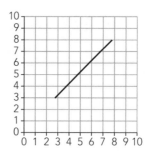

15 A population of flamingos lives in a safari park.

The graph shows how the population changed over a three-year period.

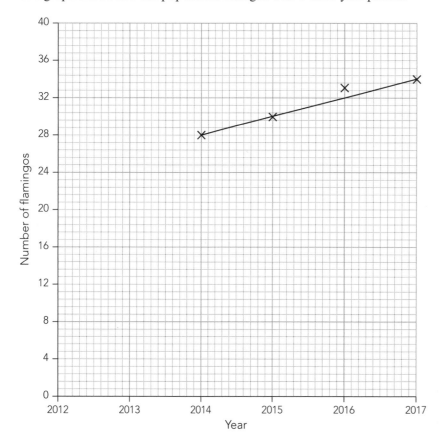

Use the graph to estimate the number of flamingos in the park in 2012.

....

16 A patient has a bacterial infection. The graph shows how the population of bacteria changed.

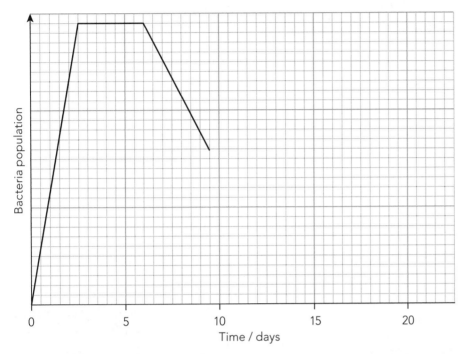

a The patient started taking an antibiotic. After how many days did the patient start taking it?

....

b Estimate the day that all the bacteria will be killed.

....

EXAM-STYLE QUESTIONS

1   A student was asked to cycle on an exercise bicycle.

The graph shows how the student's breathing rate changed.

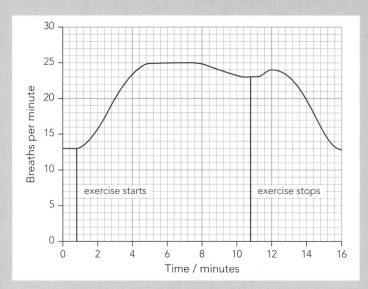

a   **State** how long the student was exercising for.

.... [1]

b   **Calculate** the increase in breathing rate from when the student started exercising to the maximum rate.

.... [2]

c   **Describe** what happened to the change in breathing rate in the final 2 minutes of exercise.

Suggest a reason for this change.

....

....   [2]

[Total: 5]

COMMAND WORDS

state: express in clear terms

calculate: work out from given facts, figures or information

describe: state the points of a topic / give characteristics and main features

suggest: apply knowledge and understanding to situations where there are a range of valid responses in order to make proposals/ put forward considerations a topic / give characteristics and main features

CONTINUED

2 Scientists estimated the number of voles living in a field over 10 years.

The graph shows the data they collected.

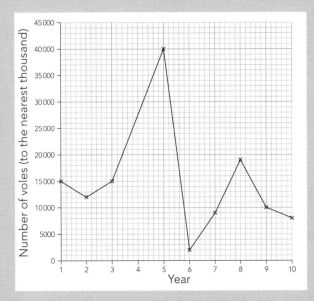

a They did not count the voles in year 4.

A student estimates that there were 27 000 voles in year 4.

Describe how she used to graph to get this answer.

.... [1]

b **Explain** why this value is not reliable.

.... [1]

[Total: 2]

COMMAND WORD

explain: set out purposes or reasons / make the relationships between things evident / provide why and/or how and support with relevant evidence

3   The scatter graph shows the relationship between two variables.

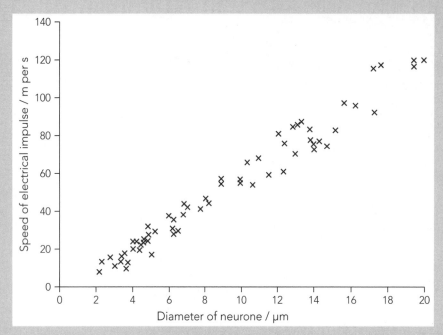

a   Name the type of correlation shown in the graph.

    ....

    [1]

b   Draw a best-fit line on the graph. Explain how the graph shows that the correlation between the variables is strong.

    ....

    ....

    [2]

c   Describe what the scatter graph shows.

    ....

    [1]

    [Total: 4]

> Chapter 5

Doing calculations

WHY DO YOU NEED TO DO CALCULATIONS IN BIOLOGY?

- You will be given information in different forms, including data and diagrams.

- Doing calculations, such as calculating percentages, ratios and scale, will help you to interpret the information.

Maths focus 1: Calculating percentages

The term 'per cent' means 1 out of 100. The symbol % is used to show a percentage.

These are some examples of percentages used in biology:

- Of all the species that have existed on Earth, 99.9% are now extinct.

- Humans share 50% of their DNA with bananas.

- Around 10% of people are left-handed.

We can use percentages to estimate proportions.

For example, if 10% of people are left-handed then in a population of 50 million people, we would expect 5 million to be left-handed.

An important part of biology is studying change. This might be a change in the mass of an organism, or a change in a variable during an investigation. Calculating percentage increase or decrease shows how much this value has changed.

What maths skills do you need to calculate percentages?

1	Calculating percentages	• Calculate the percentage of a quantity, e.g. 40% of 50.
		• Calculate a quantity as a percentage, e.g. 18 out of 72.
2	Calculating percentage change	• Calculate the difference between the numbers you are comparing: Difference = new number − original number
		• Divide the difference by the original number and multiply the number by 100: $\% \text{ change} = \left(\dfrac{\text{difference}}{\text{original number}}\right) \times 100$
		• Decide if it shows a percentage increase or decrease.

Maths skill practice

How does calculating percentages relate to organisms and their environment?

The study of organisms and how they interact with their environment is called *ecology. This topic is covered in Chapter 18 of the Coursebook.*

Animals (consumers) get the energy they need to live by eating. You can calculate a percentage to show how much of the energy in their food is used for different life processes.

The size of a population can change over time, as shown in Figure 5.1. Calculating the percentage decrease or increase will show how much the population has changed.

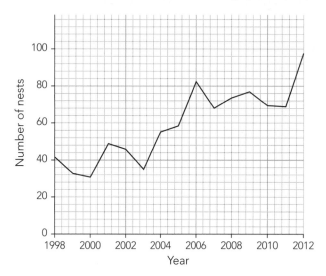

LOOK OUT
If the answer is not a percentage you may need to include a unit.

Figure 5.1: The number of barn owl nests changes over time. Can you see between which years there was a population increase and which years there was a decrease?

Maths skill 1: Calculating percentages

WORKED EXAMPLE 5.1

Some locusts ate part of a crop of maize.

The maize contained 5000 kJ of energy.

Only 10% of this energy was passed to the locusts.

Calculate the number of joules transferred to the locusts.

This question is asking you to calculate the percentage of a quantity.

Step 1: Change the percentage to a decimal by dividing it by 100:

$$\frac{10}{100} = 0.1$$

You can easily change a percentage into a decimal using place value.

To divide a number by 100, move the decimal point two place values to the left:

$$10 \div 100 = 0.1$$

$$1\,0. \rightarrow .10 = 0.1$$

For more information about place value, see Chapter 1, Maths focus 2, Representing very large and very small numbers.

Step 2: Multiply by the quantity:

$$0.1 \times 5000 = 500 \text{ kJ}$$

The answer is 500 kJ.

WORKED EXAMPLE 5.2

Figure 5.2 shows how a caterpillar transfers energy from its food.

Calculate the percentage of food used for growth.

Food 20 J

Respiration 6 J

Growth 3 J

Faeces 11 J

Figure 5.2: How a caterpillar transfers energy from its food.

The question is asking you to calculate a quantity as a percentage.

Step 1: Identify the two numbers you need to use.

This is the number of joules in its food and the number of joules used for growth.

> **CONTINUED**

So, you need to use the numbers 20 and 3.

Step 2: Divide the smaller number by the larger number.

$$\frac{3}{20} = 0.15$$

Step 3: Multiply the answer by 100.

$$0.15 \times 100 = 15\%$$

The percentage of food used for growth is 15%.

Questions

1 Calculate:

a 20% of 240 ....

b 12% of 360 ....

c 75% of 1520 ....

2 a Use Figure 5.2 to calculate the percentage of energy from food that a caterpillar loses in its faeces.

....

b Explain to a partner the steps you used to work out the answer in part **a** and why you used each one. Did your partner do anything differently?

3 Zara has a bird table in her garden.

She uses a tally chart to count how many birds of each species visit the bird table in 1 hour.

Her results are shown in the table.

Bird species	Visits in 1 hour
Common redstart	|||
Red-vented bulbul	|
Whinchat	ЖЖ |
Isabelline wheatear	||

a Calculate the total number of birds that Zara sees.

....

b What percentage of the birds were common redstarts?

....

Maths skill 2: Calculating percentage change

WORKED EXAMPLE 5.3

Table 5.1 shows how the estimated biomass of herring in the North Sea changed between 1965 and 2005.

Year	Herring biomass / thousand tonnes
1965	2035
1970	452
1975	149
1980	105
1985	743
1990	1256
1995	502
2000	954
2005	1928

Table 5.1: Change in the estimated biomass of herring in the North Sea.

Calculate the percentage change in herring biomass between 1965 and 1970.

State if it is a percentage increase or decrease.

In 1965 the herring biomass was 2035 thousand tonnes. In 1970 it was 452 thousand tonnes.

Because both numbers show thousand tonnes, you can just use the numbers 2035 and 452 in your calculation.

Step 1: Calculate the difference between the numbers you are comparing:

$$\text{Difference} = \text{new number} - \text{original number}$$

$$452 - 2035 = -1583$$

Step 2: Divide the difference by the original number and multiply the number by 100:

$$\% \text{ change} = \left(\frac{\text{difference}}{\text{original number}}\right) \times 100$$

$$\% \text{ change} = \left(\frac{-1583}{2035}\right) \times 100 = -77.8\%$$

Step 3: Decide if your answer shows a percentage increase or decrease.

The answer is a negative number, which is a percentage decrease.

The answer is a 77.8% decrease in herring biomass between 1965 and 1970.

Questions

4 Use Table 5.1 to calculate the percentage change in the biomass of herring population between 2000 and 2005.

Give your answer to one decimal place.

State if it is a percentage increase or decrease.

....

....

....

5 What parts of calculating percentage change do you find difficult?

What do you need to improve before you try the next question?

....

....

....

6 Figure 5.3 shows the number of joules in the tissues of organisms in a food chain.

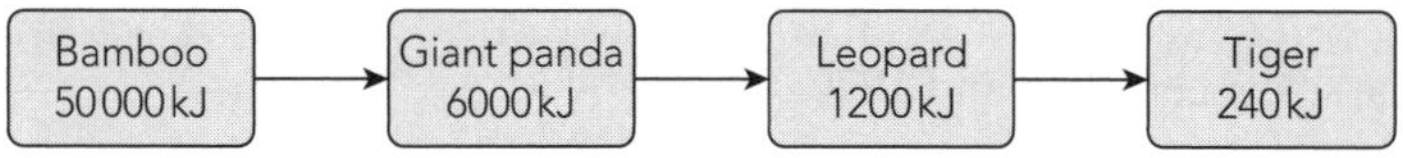

Bamboo 50 000 kJ → Giant panda 6000 kJ → Leopard 1200 kJ → Tiger 240 kJ

Figure 5.3: The number of joules along a food chain.

Calculate the percentage energy loss between:

a Bamboo and giant panda

....

....

....

b Giant panda and leopard

....

....

....

c Leopard and tiger

....

....

....

Maths focus 2: Using scale drawings and magnification

scale: a set of marks with equal intervals, for example on a graph axis or a measuring cylinder; or, on a scale diagram, the ratio of a length in the diagram to the actual size

scale drawing: a diagram in which all lengths are in the same ratio to the corresponding lengths in the actual object (to the same scale)

In biology you will often have to study objects that are very small, such as cells.

You might also study objects that are very large, such as entire habitats.

These objects are drawn as **scale drawings**, which makes the drawings a suitable size to be displayed on the page of a book or a computer screen.

In order to calculate the actual size of an object, a **scale** is used. The scale tells you the ratio of any length in the drawing to the corresponding length in the actual object.

Figure 5.4 shows an example of a scale drawing.

Figure 5.4: A scale drawing of a horse.

What maths skills do you need to use scale?

1	Interpreting scale drawings	<ul><li>Use a ruler to measure the length of the scale bar given in the drawing.</li><li>Use a ruler to measure the drawing.</li><li>Use ratios to calculate the actual size of the drawing.</li><li>Use the correct unit in the answer.</li></ul>
2	Using the magnification formula	<ul><li>Identify the magnification (it will start with a ×).</li><li>Use a ruler to measure the image in millimetres.</li><li>Use the formula: $\text{actual size} = \dfrac{\text{size of image}}{\text{magnification}}$</li></ul>

You might see ratios on scale drawings. These are rarely used in biology, but you may use them in other subjects.

In Figure 5.4, the scale ratio is 1 : 40. This means that 1 unit of length on the drawing is equal to 40 units on the actual horse. So, 1 cm on the drawing is equal to 40 cm on the actual horse.

Maths skill practice

> KEY WORD
>
> **magnification:** the factor by which something has been enlarged:
>
> $\text{magnification} = \dfrac{\text{length of image}}{\text{actual length}}$

How does using scale relate to cells?

Cells are very small. They are microscopic: this means that to view them you need a microscope to magnify them.

A typical human skin cell has a diameter of $30\,\mu m$, or $0.03\,mm$.

See Chapter 1, Maths focus 1, Using units, for information on how to convert units.

The images of cells that you see in books, such as those in *Chapter 2 of the Coursebook*, are enlarged images. They are often scale drawings, so the actual size of the cell can be calculated.

Some scale drawings will provide you with a scale bar (as in Figure 5.5a). Others will have a **magnification** (as in Figure 5.5b). Both will allow you to calculate the actual size of the cell.

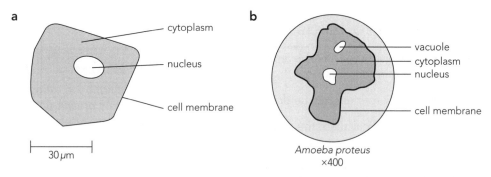

Figure 5.5: Scale drawings of cells.

Maths skill 1: Interpreting scale drawings

WORKED EXAMPLE 5.4

Figure 5.6 shows a diagram of a bacterium.

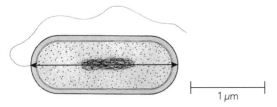

Figure 5.6: A bacterium.

What is the length of the bacterium?

Step 1: Measure the length of the scale bar.

The scale bar is 2 cm long.

This means that 2 cm on the diagram represents 1 μm.

Step 2: Measure the drawing.

The length of the bacterium in the drawing is 4 cm.

Step 3: Use ratios to calculate the actual size of the drawing.

	Size on drawing	Actual size
Scale bar	2 cm	1 μm
Length of bacterium	4 cm ×2	? ×2

So, the length of the bacterium is 2 μm.

> **LOOK OUT**
>
> Remember to include the correct units in your answer.

Questions

7   Calculate the diameter of the red blood cell below. Follow the steps above.

....

....

....

8 Calculate the diameter of the virus in the scale drawing.

....

....

....

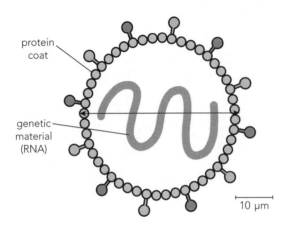

Maths skill 2: Using the magnification formula

The magnification formula is:

$$\text{actual size} = \frac{\text{size of image}}{\text{magnification}}$$

This formula can be used to calculate the actual size of an object, such as a cell, using the size of a magnified image.

The magnification will be given on the image.

A magnification of ×10 000 tells you that in the image, the object has been magnified by 10 000; it is 10 000 times bigger than in real life. Magnification is a ratio of two lengths so it has no unit.

The form of the equation used to calculate the magnification is:

$$\text{magnification} = \frac{\text{size of image}}{\text{actual size}}$$

WORKED EXAMPLE 5.5

Figure 5.7 shows cells from the trachea of a mammal.

Use the magnification formula to calculate the length of the cell marked in the image.

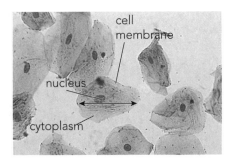

Figure 5.7: Cells from the trachea of a mammal, seen through a light microscope (×300).

Step 1: Identify the magnification (it will start with ×).

The magnification is ×300. This means that the image is 300 times larger than the real cells.

Step 2: Use a ruler to measure the image in millimetres.

The length of the marked cell is 16 mm.

Step 3: Use the formula:

$$\text{actual size} = \frac{\text{size of image}}{\text{magnification}}$$

$$\text{actual size} = \frac{16\,\text{mm}}{300}$$

The actual size of the marked cell is 0.05 mm.

You need to convert millimetres (mm) into micrometres (μm):

$$1000\,\mu m = 1\,mm$$

So:

$$0.05\,mm = 50\,\mu m$$

Questions

9   The image is a close-up of a leaf cell. It has a magnification of ×2000.

   a   Calculate the height of the cell in millimetres.

   Use the magnification formula.

   ....

   ....

   ....

   b   Which form of the magnification formula did you use? Why?

   ....

   ....

10   The following image is part of a liver cell, taken using an electron microscope.

nucleus

The magnification is ×20 000.

Calculate the diameter of the nucleus in micrometres (μm).

Use the magnification formula.

....

....

....

> **LOOK OUT**
>
> You might be asked to measure the diameter of a circular object. To do this, draw a straight line through the centre of the object.

11   A drawing of a plant cell in a textbook has a length of 10.2 cm.

   The actual plant cell has a length of 0.1 mm.

   Use the magnification formula to calculate the magnification of the image.

   $$\text{magnification} = \frac{\text{size of image}}{\text{actual size}}$$

   ....

   ....

   ....

12 A student found an electron microscope image of a mitochondrion.

The width of the mitochondrion in the image was 34 mm.

The width of a real mitochondrion is 1 μm.

Use the magnification formula to calculate the magnification of the image.

....

....

....

Maths focus 3: Understanding ratio and probability

Ratios are used in everyday life to compare amounts of something. For example, in a recipe it says to use 2 parts flour to 1 part cocoa. This means that you need to use twice as much flour compared to cocoa. This could be 50 g of flour and 25 g of cocoa or 200 g of flour and 100 g of cocoa.

In biology a scientist can use ratio and probability in genetic experiments.

For example:

A scientist grew 10 pea plants from seeds.

Six of the pea plants had white flowers.

The other four had pink flowers.

He can discuss the results in terms of:

Ratio: the ratio of white to pink flowers is 6:4.

To simplify the ratio, first work out the largest number that each amount in the ratio is divisible by. Then, divide each amount by this number. The largest number 6 and 4 can be divided by is 2, so 6:4 can be simplified to 3:2.

When you read a ratio, say 'to' for the colon (:). So, for this ratio you say 'three to two'.

Probability: if he had picked a seed at random and planted it, there would have been a 6 in 10, or 60%, chance that the plant will have white flowers and a 4 in 10, or 40%, chance that it will have pink flowers.

What maths skills do you need to calculate ratio and probability?

1	Calculating ratio	• Read the ratio you need to calculate, e.g. number of A to the number of B.
		• Write the amounts with a colon (:) in between them. Put the numbers in the correct order, so A will go first.
		• Write the ratio in its simplest form.
2	Calculating probability	• Work out the number of possible outcomes. This is y.
		• Work out the number of outcomes of interest. This is x.
		• Give the probability in the form of x in y.
		• Simplify the probability if possible.

Maths skill practice

How does calculating ratio and probability relate to inheritance?

Offspring produced by sexual reproduction share features with both parents.

This happens because chromosomes are passed from parent to offspring.

Figure 5.8 is a genetic diagram called a Punnett square. A Punnett square shows the alleles of each parent (their genotypes) plus all the possible combinations that can be produced in the offspring. You can use genetic diagrams to calculate the ratio and probability of different genotypes and phenotypes in the offspring.

You can read more about Punnett squares, and get some more practice at drawing them, by referring to Chapter 16 in the Coursebook.

Female gametes

		G	g
Male gametes	G	GG *Grey*	Gg *Grey*
	g	Gg *Grey*	gg *Black*

Figure 5.8: A Punnett square which shows the possible combinations of alleles for fur colour from two parent cats G = grey fur allele, g = black fur allele.

The phenotype is fur colour, which can be grey or black. The Punnett square shows that there are four possible combinations of alleles. Three of these result in the phenotype grey fur, and one results in black fur.

Maths skill 1: Calculating ratio

A *ratio* is a way of comparing amounts of something.

WORKED EXAMPLE 5.6

Marcus found Figure 5.9 in a textbook.
It is a genetic diagram.

It shows how flower colour is inherited in pea plants.

What is the ratio of possible combinations of alleles in these offspring of:

a red to white flowers

b homozygous to heterozygous genotypes?

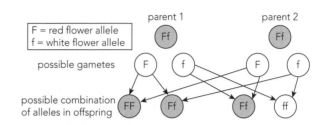

Figure 5.9: A genetic diagram showing alleles for red and white flowers.

Part a   Here are the steps you should take:

Step 1: Read the ratio you need to calculate, e.g. number of A to the number of B.

Part **a** asks for the ratio of red to white flowers.

Three of the combinations result in red flowers, and one in white flowers.

Step 2: Write the amounts with a colon (:) in between them.
Put the numbers in the correct order, so A will go first: 3:1

Step 3: Write the ratio in its simplest form.

The largest number both amounts can be divided by is 1, so 3:1 is the simplest form of the ratio.

The ratio of red to white flowers is 3:1.

This is called the phenotypic ratio.

This ratio shows there are three red flowers to every one white flower.

Part b   Two of the combinations have a homozygous genotype (FF or ff) and two have a heterozygous genotype (Ff).

The ratio of homozygous genotype to heterozygous is 2:2.

Both sides of the ratio are divisible by 2, so it can be simplified to give a ratio of 1:1.

The ratio of homozygous to heterozygous genotypes is 1:1.

This ratio shows that there are an equal number of homozygous and heterozygous genotypes in the combinations.

Ratios can be used to make predictions.

For example, in this example the ratio of red to white flowers is 3:1.

If 100 seeds from this cross were grown, then you would expect there to be around 75 red plants and 25 white plants.

LOOK OUT

The largest amount is not always written first. If the question asked for the ratio of white to red flowers, then the answer would be 1:3.

Questions

13 a A litter of kittens contains three with short hair and two with long hair. What is the ratio of short to long haired kittens?

....

b In a group of 10 fruit flies, seven have red eyes and the rest have white eyes. Write this as a ratio of red eyes to white eyes.

....

14 Work in small group. Think of a question that can be answered with a yes or no. It should get a good mix of answers from a group of people. For example, 'Do you have a brother?' Ask the class your question and count up how many people said yes and how many people said no. Calculate this as a ratio. Repeat this for the questions other groups in your class ask.

15 Simplify these ratios:

a $10:5$

....

b $4:16$

....

c $9:3$

....

d $40:120$

....

16 The following genetic diagram shows a cross between two cats.

Female gametes

		g	g
Male gametes	G	Gg Grey fur	Gg Grey fur
	g	gg Black fur	gg Black fur

a What is the expected ratio of grey to black fur in the offspring?

....

b Write down the steps you used to answer this question.

....

....

....

Maths skill 2: Calculating probability

Probability shows how likely it is that an event will occur.

If you toss a coin, then there are two possible outcomes: heads or tails.

Each time you toss a coin the probability of getting a head is 1 in 2. The probability of getting a tail is also 1 in 2.

Genetic diagrams show us all the possible combinations of alleles that can form in the offspring. In the genetic diagrams you will use, there will always be a total of four possible combinations.

Probability can be used to show how likely the different combinations are.

WORKED EXAMPLE 5.7

Cystic fibrosis (cf) is a genetic illness caused by two recessive alleles, aa.

Figure 5.10 is a genetic diagram that shows the cross between two parents who are carriers for cystic fibrosis.

		Female gametes	
		A	a
Male gametes	A	AA *Do not have cf*	Aa *Carrier of cf*
	a	Aa *Carrier of cf*	aa *Have cf*

Figure 5.10: A genetic cross to show the possible combination of alleles from two parents who are carriers of cystic fibrosis.

What is the probability that a child born from the parents in Figure 5.10 will:

a   have cystic fibrosis

b   not have cystic fibrosis

c   be a carrier of cystic fibrosis

d   not have cystic fibrosis or be a carrier?

Key questions to ask yourself:

1   How many possible outcomes are there?

   There are always four combinations of alleles in the Punnett square, so there are four possible outcomes.

2   How many of those combinations will result in the outcome in the question?

   Look at the alleles. For example, it shows you that the combination of AA will result in a child not having cystic fibrosis.

3   How do you show the probability of an offspring having this combination?

   Show the probability as a number out of 4. For example, there is only one AA. So the probability of an offspring having AA is 1 in 4.

CONTINUED

a The genotype for this phenotype is aa.
There is one aa in the cross.

Probability = 1 in 4

b The genotypes for this phenotype are AA and Aa.

Probability = 3 in 4

c The genotype for this phenotype is Aa.

Probability = 2 in 4

Both numbers can be divided by 2 so this is simplified to 1 in 2.

d The genotype for this phenotype is AA

Probability = 1 in 4

These probabilities show the likelihood of each phenotype each time the parents have a baby. It does not show the exact numbers. For example, if the parents had four children then we might expect one baby to have cystic fibrosis, but in reality it could be none or more than one.

LOOK OUT

Probability can also be shown as a percentage, fraction or decimal number. For example, 1 in 2 can also be written as 50%, $\frac{1}{2}$ or 0.5.

Questions

17 Huntington's disease is an example of a genetic illness. If you have the dominant allele, H, you have the illness.

The following genetic cross shows the possible outcomes from a woman who has the disease and a man who does not.

		Female gametes	
		H	h
Male gametes	h	Hh Has illness	hh Healthy
	h	Hh Has illness	hh Healthy

a Calculate the probability of the couple having a child with the illness.

Give your answer as a percentage.

....

b What would this probability be if the woman has the genotype HH?

....

18 Sex is inherited through sex chromosomes, X and Y.

Females have two X chromosomes and males have one X and one Y chromosome.

Use the following genetic cross to show why the probability of having a baby boy is 1 in 2.

		Female gametes	
		X	X
Male gametes	X	XX	XX
	Y	XY	XY

....

....

EXAM-STYLE QUESTIONS

1 The image of the cheek cell shown has a magnification of ×100.
The width of the cell is shown by the line.

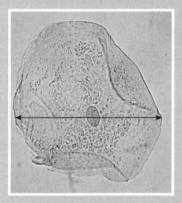

a **Calculate** the actual size of the cell in millimetres.

Use the formula: actual size $= \dfrac{\text{size of image}}{\text{magnification}}$

....

.... [1]

b Convert this width into micrometres (μm).

....

.... [1]

c A red blood cell has a diameter of 8 μm.
A bacterial cell is 40 times smaller.
Calculate the diameter of a bacterial cell.

.... [1]

[Total: 3]

COMMAND WORD

calculate: work out from given facts, figures or information

CONTINUED

2   Blood is a tissue made up of many different components.

The diagram shows the percentage of each component, by volume, in a sample of blood.

Plasma (55%)
White blood cells and platelets (1%)
Red blood cells

a   Calculate the percentage of red blood cells in blood.

....

.... [1]

b   Calculate the volume of plasma in a 156 cm³ sample of blood.

....

.... [2]

[Total: 3]

3   A patient had a blood test. The table shows the number of the different blood cells per cm³ in the patient's blood.

Blood component	Number per cm³
platelets	250 000 000
white blood cells	3 200 000
red blood cells	5 000 000 000

a   Calculate the ratio of red blood cells to platelets.

....

....

.... [3]

b   A month later the patient has another blood test. The results show they have 2 400 000 white blood cells per cm³ of blood. Calculate the percentage change in the number of white blood cells.

....

....

.... [3]

[Total: 6]

> Chapter 6

Working with shape

WHY DO YOU NEED TO WORK WITH SHAPE IN BIOLOGY?

- Some of the two-dimensional (2D) shapes you will come across in biology are squares, oblongs and circles.

- Some of the three-dimensional (3D) shapes you will come across are cubes and rectangular blocks.

- You might be asked to calculate the area or surface area of a shape.

Maths focus: Calculating area

KEY WORDS

area: a measure of the size of a surface (measured in square units; e.g. cm^2 or m^2)

cube: a three-dimensional object that has six square faces

oblong: a shape that has two long sides of equal length and two short sides of equal length

square: a shape with four sides of equal length

surface area: the total area of surface of a three-dimensional object

Area is a measurement of the surface of an object.

In biology you will need to be able to calculate the area of circles as well as the **surface area** of **cubes**.

129 >

What maths skills do you need to calculate area?

1	Calculating the surface area of a cube and a rectangular block	**Cube** • Calculate the area of one **square** face. • There are six faces so multiply the area of one face by 6. **Rectangular block** • Calculate the area of each side (they could be squares or **oblongs**). • Add the six areas together.
2	Calculating the area of a circle	• The formula used is: area $= \pi r^2$ • Use a ruler to measure the radius of the circle. • Square the radius (multiply it by itself). • Multiply the squared radius by π.

Maths skill practice

KEY WORDS

circumference: the distance around a circle

radius: the distance from the centre of a circle (or sphere) to the circumference (or sphere surface)

How does calculating area relate to investigations in biology?

Circles

You might calculate the area of circles when looking at how effective different chemicals, such as antibiotics, are against bacteria.

The bacteria are grown on a jelly called agar in a Petri dish. Small paper discs that have been soaked in an antibiotic are placed on the agar. After the bacteria have grown, there will be clear circular regions around the effective antibiotics (see Figure 6.1). The area of these regions (called zones of inhibition) can be calculated to find out which antibiotic was the most effective. The larger the area of the circle, the more effective the antibiotic.

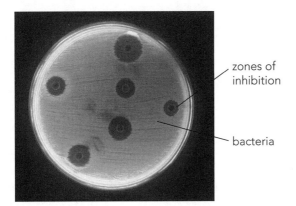

Figure 6.1: The antibiotics diffuse from the paper discs and prevent bacteria from growing. This forms circular zones of inhibition.

Surface area of cubes

Some substances move in and out of cells by diffusion through the cell membrane.

Surface area is a factor that affects the rate of diffusion: the larger the surface area of an object, the faster diffusion happens.

You might investigate this by using cubes of agar. By cutting up a cube into smaller cubes you can increase the surface area (while keeping the overall volume the same). You then measure how long it takes for a substance to diffuse into the centre of the cubes. *This experiment is covered in Chapter 3 of the Coursebook.*

Figure 6.2: Cutting a large cube into smaller cubes increases the surface area and increases the rate of diffusion.

Maths skill 1: Calculating the surface area of a cube and a rectangular block

A cube has six sides. Each side has the same area.

The area of one side is calculated by multiplying the length of a side by itself, $a \times a$ or a^2; see Figure 6.3.

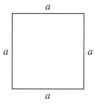

Figure 6.3: The area of a square is a × a.

The surface area of a cube is calculated by adding up the areas of its sides.

A cube has six sides; see Figure 6.4. So, a cube with a side length of 1 cm will have a surface area of 6 cm².

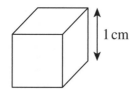

1 cm

Figure 6.4: This cube will have a surface area of 6 cm².

You can also calculate the surface area of a rectangular block (Figure 6.5).

Figure 6.5: A rectangular block has three pairs of sides. The sides in each pair are opposite each other. Both sides in a pair have the same area.

To calculate the surface area of a rectangular block:

Calculate the area of any square sides, using the method above.

Then calculate the area of each oblong side. Multiply the length of a long side by the length of a short side, a × b (Figure 6.6). Finally, add all the areas together.

b

a

Figure 6.6: The area of an oblong is a × b.

Common units of length used in biology are millimetres (mm), centimetres (cm), metres (m) and kilometres (km).

Units of area are mm², cm², m² and km².

You can find out more about units in Chapter 1, Representing values.

Many students make the same mistake when converting units of area.

For example, they may think that $1\,\text{cm}^2$ is equal to $10\,\text{mm}^2$ because $1\,\text{cm} = 10\,\text{mm}$.

However, as you can see in Figure 6.7, this is not correct. A square with a side of $1\,\text{cm}$ contains $100\ (10 \times 10)$ squares with a side of $1\,\text{mm}$. So, $1\,\text{cm}^2 = 100\,\text{mm}^2$.

To convert the units of area you must square the multiplier used for the conversion of length:

$$\text{mm} \to \text{cm}\ (\times 10)$$
$$\text{mm}^2 \to \text{cm}^2\ (\times 10^2)$$

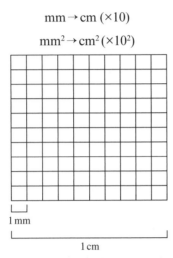

1 mm

1 cm

Figure 6.7: An area of $1\,\text{cm}^2$ equals $100\,\text{mm}^2$.

WORKED EXAMPLE 6.1

Calculate the surface area of the cube in Figure 6.8. Give your answer in mm^2.

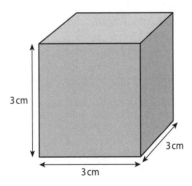

3 cm

3 cm

3 cm

Figure 6.8: A cube.

Step 1: Make sure the units of length are correct. If not, convert them.

The sides are 3 cm long. The area needs to be given in mm².

3 cm = 3 × 10 = 30 mm

CONTINUED

Step 2: Calculate area by squaring the length of one side.

$30^2 = 900$

Step 3: Calculate the surface area by multiplying the area of one side by 6.

$900 \times 6 = 5400$

Step 4: Use the correct unit for the area. This is mm^2.

$5400\,mm^2$

LOOK OUT

It is easier to convert the units of length, rather than area, so convert the length first before calculating the area.

Questions

1 The length of the sides of a cube is 5 cm.

    a Calculate the area of one side in cm^2.

    ....

    b Calculate the surface area of the cube.

    ....

    c Ask a partner to check your answers to parts **a** and **b** and underline any part of the calculation they think you did incorrectly. Look again at your answer before moving on.

2 Zara wanted to make a cube of agar with a surface area of $54\,cm^2$.

How long do the sides of the cube need to be?

Give your answer in mm.

....

....

....

LOOK OUT

The opposite of squaring a number is calculating the square root. You can use the symbol √ on your calculator to find the square root of a number.

3 Arun was investigating osmosis.

Arun cut pieces of potato into rectangular blocks, as shown.

    1.2 cm
    1.2 cm
    5.5 cm

    a Write down the steps Arun should use to calculate the surface area of the block.

    ....

    ....

    ....

b Calculate the surface area of the block.

....

....

....

c Discuss with a partner why calculating the surface area of a rectangular block is different to calculating the surface area of a cube.

Maths skill 2: Calculating the area of a circle

The formula used to calculate the area of a circle is:

$$area = \pi \times radius^2$$

This can be shortened to:

$$A = \pi r^2$$

See Figure 6.9 for the parts of a circle: **radius**, diameter and **circumference**.

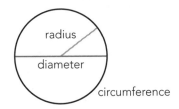

Figure 6.9: The radius is the distance between the centre of the circle and the circumference. The diameter is twice the radius.

π is the symbol for the Greek letter pi. It is pronounced 'pie'. Its value is 3.14 to three significant figures. See Chapter 1, Representing values, for more about significant figures.

> **LOOK OUT**
>
> You will have a π button on your calculator which gives you the number not rounded. Use this button in calculations to give a more accurate answer.

> **WORKED EXAMPLE 6.2**

Zara wanted to see which antibiotic was most effective against a strain of bacteria.

She spread bacteria over agar jelly in a Petri dish and added three discs that had each been soaked in a different antibiotic. She labelled the antibiotics A, B and C (see Figure 6.10a).

Zara left the dish in a warm place. Figure 6.10b shows the dish after 24 hours.

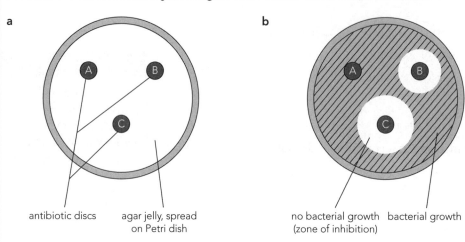

a

b

antibiotic discs · agar jelly, spread on Petri dish

no bacterial growth (zone of inhibition) · bacterial growth

Figure 6.10: a The dish before bacterial growth. **b** The dish after growth.

Zara wanted to measure the area of the zone of inhibition around disc B.

These are the steps to take:

Step 1: Use a ruler to measure the radius of the circle (Figure 6.11).

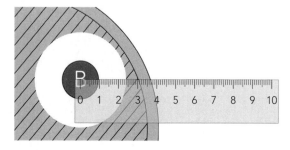

Figure 6.11: Measuring the radius.

The radius is 2.4 cm.

Step 2: Square the radius (multiply it by itself).

2.4 × 2.4 = 5.76

CONTINUED

Step 3: Multiply the radius by π. Find this on your calculator.

$$5.76 \times \pi = 18.1$$

Step 4: Use the correct unit for the area.

$$18.1\,cm^2$$

LOOK OUT

If you are not told the radius of a circle you can also calculate it by dividing the diameter in half.

Questions

4 The radius of the zone of inhibition around disc C in Figure 6.10b is 4.4 cm.

Use the formula $A = \pi r^2$ to calculate the area of the zone of inhibition.

....

5 The diameter of a Petri dish is 90 mm.

Use the formula $A = \pi r^2$ to calculate the area of the Petri dish in centimetres.

Give your answer to three significant figures.

....

....

6 Draw a circle on a piece of paper (use a compass to make sure it is an exact circle) or draw one on a computer and print it out.

a Calculate the area of your circle. Write this on the back of the piece of paper.

b As a class, place your circles around the classroom. Choose a time, such as 5 minutes. Go around the classroom and calculate the area of each circle. Check your answers. How many did you get correct in the time limit? How does this compare to others?

EXAM-STYLE QUESTIONS

1   A student investigated how the surface area of a cube affected the
    rate of diffusion.

    The student made two cubes of the same size out of agar jelly.

    The student cut one cube into eight smaller cubes of equal size.

    This is shown in the diagram.

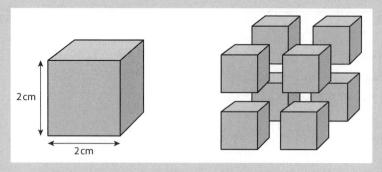

  a **Calculate** the surface area of the large cube.

   ....

   ....

   .... [2]

  b Calculate the total surface area of the small cubes.

   ....

   ....

   .... [3]

  c **Predict** how cutting the cube up into smaller cubes will affect the
   rate of diffusion. **Give** a reason for your prediction.

   ....

   ....

   .... [2]

                            [Total: 7]

COMMAND WORDS

calculate: work out
from given facts,
figures or information

predict: suggest
what may
happen based on
available information

give: produce
an answer from a
given source or
recall/memory

CONTINUED

2 A scientist investigated the effect of a cleaning liquid on bacteria.

The diagram shows the way the scientist set up the investigation.

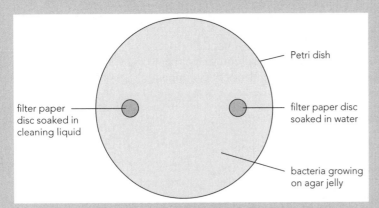

The scientist put the Petri dish in an incubator at 25 °C for 48 hours.

After 48 hours, the scientist measured the diameter of the clear circle around each disc. The results are shown in the table.

Disc	Diameter of clear circle around the disc / cm
water	0
cleaning liquid	2.4

Use the formula $A = \pi r^2$ to calculate the area of the clear circle around the cleaning liquid. Give your answer to three significant figures.

....

....

.... [3]

[Total: 3]

3 The diagram shows an overhead view of a lake.
Use the grid to estimate the area of the lake.

.... [1]

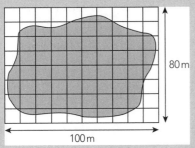

✔ These squares are included.

✘ These squares are not included.

[Total: 1]

LOOK OUT

To estimate an area using a grid, count up the squares that are completely covered. For partially covered squares, only count the ones that are covered by half or more.

> Applying more than one skill

Exam-style questions and sample answers have been written by the authors. References to assessment and/or assessment preparation are the publisher's interpretation of the syllabus requirements and may not fully reflect the approach of Cambridge Assessment International Education.

In examinations, the way in which marks are awarded may be different.

1   A student investigated how temperature affects the rate of diffusion.

   The diagram shows the equipment he used.

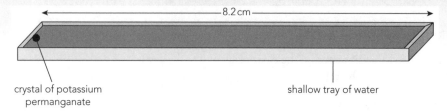

crystal of potassium permanganate

shallow tray of water

   He filled the tray with cold water and measured the time it took for colour from the potassium permanganate to reach the end of the tray. It took 122 s.

   He then repeated this with warm and then hot water.

   The bar chart shows the results.

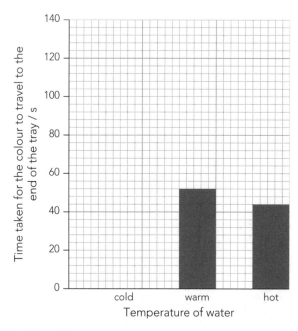

   a   Draw the bar for cold water.   [1]

b State how long it took for the colour to travel to the end in the warm water.

.... [1]

c Calculate the rate of movement for the colour in hot water. Give your answer in mm/s to two significant figures.

....

.... [2]

d The teacher asked the student to change his method so he could draw a line graph.

Describe how he should do this.

.... [2]

[Total: 6]

2 A scientist viewed red blood cells under a microscope and measured their diameter.

The average diameter of a red blood cell was 8 µm.

a Convert this measurement into mm.

.... [2]

The scientist then placed the red blood cells into sodium chloride solution.

The photo shows a microscope image of the red blood cells after 30 minutes.

The magnification used was ×4000.

b Calculate the diameter of the red blood cell in µm.

Use the formula:

$$\text{actual size} = \frac{\text{size of image}}{\text{magnification}}$$

....

.... [3]

c The average diameter of the blood cells before being placed in the solution was 8 µm.

The average diameter of the red blood cells after 30 minutes in the sodium chloride solution was 6 µm.

Calculate the percentage change in the average diameter of the red blood cells.

....

.... [3]

[Total: 8]

3 A student wanted to estimate the number of stomata on the bottom of some leaves.

She first needed to estimate the area of a whole leaf.

She put a leaf on a piece of squared paper and drew around it.

Each square on the paper has an area of $5\,mm^2$.

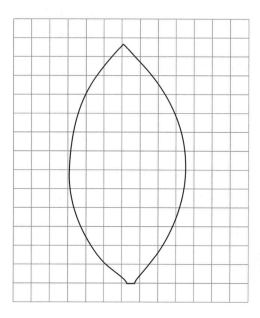

a Use the diagram to estimate the area of the leaf.

.... [1]

b Describe what she could change about the squared paper she used to make her answer more accurate.

.... [1]

The student used a more accurate method to measure the area of another leaf. The area was $525\,mm^2$.

The student used a microscope to count the number of stomata on the bottom of the leaf. She counted five stomata in an area of $0.001\,mm^2$.

c   Use a calculation to estimate the number of stomata on the bottom
of the whole leaf. Give your answer in standard form.

....

....

....

.... **[3]**

[Total: 5]

4   A group of students wanted to investigate how the concentration of sugar
affected osmosis in blocks of potato.

The students cut five blocks of potato to the same dimensions.

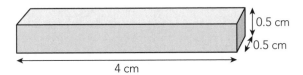

a   Calculate the surface area of one potato block.

....

.... **[2]**

The students measured the mass of each block and put each block into
a sugar solution with a different concentration.

The blocks were left for 10 minutes, and then removed from the solutions
and dried.

The students then measured the mass of each block.

The results are shown in the table.

Concentration of sugar solution / mol per dm³	Starting mass / g	Final mass / g	Change in mass / g	Percentage change
0	1.32	1.53	0.21	15.9
0.2	1.35	1.50	0.15	X
0.4	1.30	1.35	0.05	3.8
0.6	1.34	1.25	−0.09	−6.7
0.8	1.32	1.21	−0.11	−8.3

b   Calculate the missing percentage change, X.

....

.... **[2]**

c   Explain why calculating the percentage change in mass is more useful than just the change in mass in grams.

....

.... **[2]**

d   On the graph paper below, draw a graph to show the students' results:

   •   Label the *x*-axis

   •   Plot the percentage change in mass

   •   Circle the anomalous result.   **[3]**

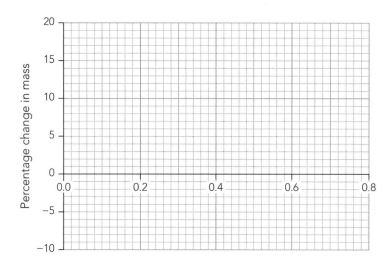

e   Draw a best-fit line.   **[1]**

                                                                        [Total: 10]

5   Polydactyly is a genetic disorder that leads to extra fingers or toes.
    Polydactyly is caused by a dominant allele, D.

    Two parents have a child who does not have polydactyly. The mother has polydactyly. The father does not.

    Calculate the probability that their next child will have polydactyly.

    Use a genetic diagram.

.... **[3]**

                                                                        [Total: 3]

6 A football coach measured the resting heart rate of his players.

    a The coach counted the number of heart beats in 15 seconds.

      Explain how the coach could convert this into beats per minute.

      .... [1]

The bar chart shows the results.

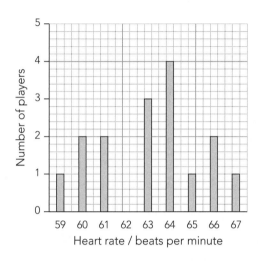

    b Four students had a heart rate of 62 beats per minute. Draw a bar to show this. [1]

    c Calculate the mean heart rate of the players.

      ....

      .... [2]

                                                                                       [Total: 4]

7 A scientist wanted to investigate how temperature affected the rate of aerobic respiration in yeast.

The equation for this reaction is:

$$\text{glucose} + \text{oxygen} \rightarrow \text{carbon dioxide} + \text{water}$$

This is the method the scientist used:

1 Use five test-tubes.

2 Place $2\,\text{cm}^3$ of glucose solution and $3\,\text{cm}^3$ of yeast suspension into each test-tube.

3 Place each test-tube into a water-bath at a different temperature: $0\,°C$, $10\,°C$, $20\,°C$, $30\,°C$ and $40\,°C$.

4 After 5 minutes add $2\,\text{cm}^3$ of methylene blue to each test-tube. Methylene blue is a dye that turns colourless when oxygen is removed.

5 Shake each tube and put it back into the water-bath. Time how long it takes for the blue colour to disappear.

The diagram shows the equipment used.

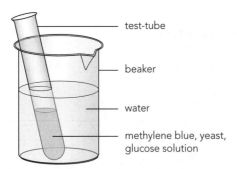

a   State the measuring instrument the scientist should use in step 5.

.... [1]

b   The scientist used syringes that had a maximum volume of $5\,cm^3$
    in steps 2 and 4.

    Explain why the scientist chose this measuring instrument.

    ....

    .... [2]

c   The scientist collected the results and drew a line graph.

    State the letter of the line that shows the results **and** explain why you chose
    this line in terms of the rate of respiration.

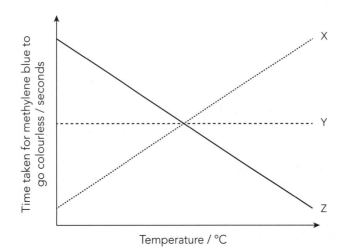

    Line ....   Reason ....

    ....

    .... [4]

[Total: 7]

8   In 2014 scientists studied the blood group of 10 000 people across all regions
    in India. The pie chart shows the results.

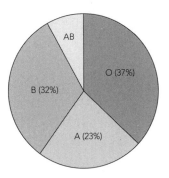

a   Calculate the percentage of people who had the blood group AB.

    .... [1]

b   In 2014 the total human population of India was approximately 1.3×10^9.

    Estimate the number of people who had blood group A. Give your answer in
    standard form.

    ....

    .... [2]

The graph shows how the population of India has changed in the last 70 years.

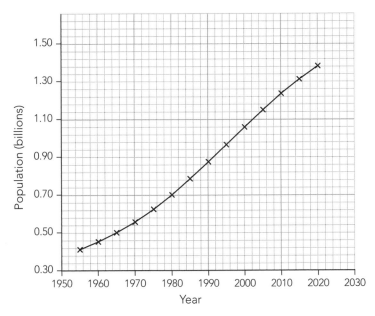

c   Estimate the population in 1998.

    .... [1]

d   Predict the population in 2030.

    .... [1]

                                                                    [Total: 5]

9   A student uses a potometer to investigate how the number of leaves on a leafy shoot affects the rate of transpiration.

The diagram shows the apparatus the student uses.

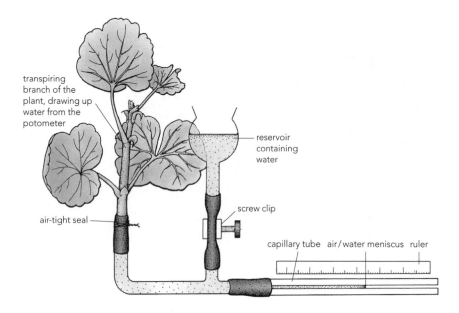

transpiring branch of the plant, drawing up water from the potometer

reservoir containing water

screw clip

air-tight seal

capillary tube   air/water meniscus   ruler

a   State one environmental factor that the student should keep constant during the investigation.

.... [1]

b   In one experiment the air bubble moved 6 mm in 20 minutes. The diameter of the capillary tube is 1.0 mm.

Calculate the rate of water uptake by the shoot.

Use this formula: volume of a cylinder = $\pi \times$ (radius of circle)$^2 \times$ height

Give your answer in mm^3 per hour to three significant figures.

....

....

.... [4]

[Total: 5]

10 A scientist used a microscope to view a cross-section of a blood vessel called an arteriole.

The image shows what the scientist saw using a magnification of ×50.

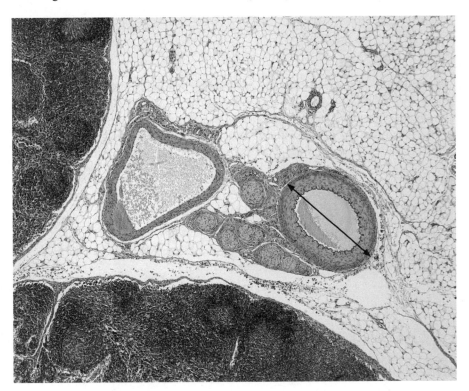

   a   Use the line on the diagram to measure the diameter of the image of the arteriole in mm.

.... [1]

   b   Calculate the actual diameter of the arteriole in mm.

Use the formula:

$$\text{actual size} = \frac{\text{size of image}}{\text{magnification}}$$

....

.... [2]

   c   Suggest how the scientist could make a more accurate measurement of the diameter of the arteriole.

....

.... [2]

[Total: 5]

> Glossary

Command Words

Below are the Cambridge International definitions for command words that may be used in exams. The information in this section is taken from the Cambridge IGCSE™ Biology syllabus (0610/0970) for examination from 2023. You should always refer to the appropriate syllabus document for the year of your examination to confirm the details and for more information. The syllabus document is available on the Cambridge International website www.cambridgeinternational.org.

calculate: work out from given facts, figures or information

compare: identify/comment on similarities and/or differences

define: give precise meaning

describe: state the points of a topic / give characteristics and main features

determine: establish an answer using the information available

evaluate: judge or calculate the quality, importance, amount, or value of something

explain: set out purposes or reasons / make the relationships between things evident / provide why and/or how and support with relevant evidence

give: produce an answer from a given source or recall/memory

identify: name/select/recognise

outline: set out main points

predict: suggest what may happen based on available information

sketch: make a simple freehand drawing showing the key features, taking care over proportions

state: express in clear terms

suggest: apply knowledge and understanding to situations where there are a range of valid responses in order to make proposals/put forward considerations

Key Words

accurate: a value that is close to the true value

anomalous result: (1) one of a series of repeated experimental results that is much larger or smaller than the others (2) a point on a graph that is considered unusual compared with the trend of other values

area: a measure of the size of a surface (measured in square units; e.g. cm^2 or m^2)

axis: a reference line on a graph or chart, along which a distance scale represents values of a variable

bar chart: a chart with separated rectangular bars of equal width; the height (or length) of a bar represents the value of the variable

best-fit line: a straight line or a smooth curve drawn on a graph that passes through or close to as many as possible of the data points; it represents the best estimate of the relationship between the variables

categorical data: data that can be grouped into categories (types) but not ordered

circumference: the distance around a circle

class: group of ordered data in a frequency table or on a histogram

continuous data: data that can take any numerical value within a range

control variable: a variable that is kept constant in an investigation

coordinates: values that determine the position of a data point on a graph, relative to the axes

correlation: a measure of the closeness of the relationship between two variables; it may be **positive** (one variable increases when the other increases) or **negative** (one variable decreases when the other increases)

cube: a three-dimensional object that has six square faces

decimal place: the place-value position of a number after a decimal point; the number 6.357 has three decimal places

dependent variable: the variable that is measured or observed in an investigation, when the independent variable is changed

derived unit: a unit made up of other units; for example, concentration can be measured in grams per cm^3 (g/cm^3)

diameter: a straight line connecting two points on the outer edge of a circle (or sphere) that passes through the centre

directly proportional: the relationship between two variables such that when one doubles (or is multiplied by n), the other variable doubles (or is multiplied by n); the graph of the two variables is a straight line through the origin

discrete data: data that can take only certain values

distribution: the way in which values in a data set are spread between the lowest and highest values

estimate: (find) an approximate value

extrapolation: extending the best-fit line on a graph beyond the range of the data, in order to estimate values not within the data set

frequency: the number of times an event occurs or number of objects/people with a certain characteristic

frequency table: a table showing the frequency of occurrence of certain categories or classes of data

gradient: the slope (steepness) of a line on a graph; it is calculated by dividing the vertical change by the horizontal change

histogram: a chart with bars showing the distribution of data that is grouped into classes; if the class intervals are equal, the height of a bar is proportional to the frequency of the class

independent variable: a variable in an investigation that is changed by the experimenter

index: a small number that indicates the power; for example, the index 4 here shows that the 2 is raised to the power 4, which means four 2s multiplied together: $2^4 = 2 \times 2 \times 2 \times 2$

intercept: the point at which a line on a graph crosses one of the axes; it usually refers to the intercept with the vertical (y-) axis

interpolation: on a graph, to estimate the value of a variable from the value of the other variable, using a best-fit line; on a scale, to estimate a measurement that falls between two scale marks

line graph: a graph of one variable against another where the data points fall on, or close to, a single line, which may be straight, curved or straight-line segments between points, depending on the relationship between the variables

magnification: the factor by which something has been enlarged:
$$\text{magnification} = \frac{\text{length of image}}{\text{actual length}}$$

mean: an average value; the sum of a set of values divided by the number of values in the set

meniscus: the curved surface of a liquid in a tube or cylinder

negative correlation: when one variable decreases as the other increases

oblong: a shape that has two long sides of equal length and two short sides of equal length

origin: the point on a graph at which the value of both variables is zero and where the axes cross

percentage: a fraction expressed out of 100 (e.g. $\frac{1}{2} = \frac{50}{100} = 50\%$)

pie chart: a circular chart that is divided into sectors which represent the relative values of components; the angle of the sector is proportional to the value of the component

positive correlation: when one variable increases as the other increases

power: a number raised to the power 2 is squared (e.g. x^2), a number raised to the power 3 is cubed (e.g. x^3), and so on

power of ten: a number such as 10^3 or 10^{-3}

precision: the closeness of agreement between several measured values obtained by repeated measurements; the precision of a single value can be indicated by the number of significant figures given in the number, for example 4.027 has greater precision (is more precise) than 4.0

qualitative data: data that are descriptive and not numerical

quantitative data: data that are numerical

radius: the distance from the centre of a circle (or sphere) to the circumference (or sphere surface)

range: the interval between a lowest value and a highest value; for example, of a measured variable or on the scale of a measuring instrument

rate: a measure of how much one variable changes relative to another variable; usually how quickly a variable changes as time progresses

ratio: a comparison of two numbers or of two measurements with the same unit; the ratio of A to B can be written A : B or expressed as a fraction $\frac{A}{B}$

rounding: expressing a number as an approximation, with fewer significant figures; for example, 7.436 rounded to two significant figure is 7.4, or rounded to three significant figures it is 7.44

scale: a set of marks with equal intervals, for example on a graph axis or a measuring cylinder; or, on a scale diagram, the ratio of a length in the diagram to the actual size

scale drawing: a diagram in which all lengths are in the same ratio to the corresponding lengths in the actual object (to the same scale)

scatter graph: a graph of one variable against another, which may or may not show a correlation between the two variables

significant figures: the number of digits in a number, not including any zeros at the beginning; for example, the number of significant figures in 0.0682 is three

square: a shape with four sides of equal length

standard form: notation in which a number is written as a number between 1 and 10 multiplied by a power of ten; for example, 4.78×10^9; also called scientific notation or standard index form

symbol: a shorter version of a unit name; for example, cm is the symbol for centimetre

surface area: the total area of surface of a three-dimensional object

trend: a pattern shown by data; on a graph this may be shown by points following a 'trend line', the best estimate of this being the best-fit line

uncertainty: the range of variation in experimental results because of sources of error; the true value is expected to be within this range

unit: a standard used in measuring a variable; for example, the metre or the volt

unit prefix: a prefix (term added to the front of a word) added to a unit name to indicate a power of 10 of that unit (e.g. 1 millimetre = 10^{-3} metre)

variable: a factor that is measured, changed or controlled in an experiment

volume: a measure of three-dimensional space; measured in cubic units, for example cm^3 or m^3

> Acknowledgements

The authors and publishers acknowledge the following sources of copyright material and are grateful for the permissions granted. While every effort has been made, it has not always been possible to identify the sources of all the material used, or to trace all copyright holders. If any omissions are brought to our notice, we will be happy to include the appropriate acknowledgements on reprinting.

Thanks to the following for permission to reproduce images:

Cover Martin Kyburz/EyeEm/Getty Images; *Inside* Carlos Aranguiz/ Getty Images; Jubal Harshaw/Shutterstock; Roberto Moiola/Sysaworld/ Getty Images; Joao Paulo Burini/ Getty Images; Sigrid Gombert/ Getty Images; andresr/ Getty Images; GlobalP/ Getty Images; Ed Reschke/ Getty Images; BIOPHOTO ASSOCIATES/SPL; Ed Reschke/ Getty Images; Smith Collection/Gado/ Getty Images; DivinHX/ Shutterstock; Jose Luis Calvo/Shutterstock